184

VOICES of FREEDOM

English and Civics

Third Edition

Bill Bliss with **Steven J. Molinsky**

Longman

longman.com

Voices of Freedom: English and Civics, Third Edition

Dedicated to Benjamin and Flora Bliss, Nathan and Sophia Bliss, and Nat and Betty Meister.

Pearson Education, 10 Bank Street, White Plains, NY 10606

Vice president, director of publishing: *Allen Ascher*
Editorial manager: *Pam Fishman*
Vice president, director of design and production: *Rhea Banker*
Director of electronic production: *Aliza Greenblatt*
Production manager: *Ray Keating*
Senior manufacturing manager: *Patrice Fraccio*
Manufacturing supervisor: *Dave Dickey*
Photo research: *Aerin Csigay*
Cover and text design: *Wendy Wolf*
Digital layout specialist: *Wendy Wolf*
Editorial supervisor: *Janet Johnston*
"A Better Life" words and music: *Peter S. Bliss*

Photo Credits

Page **1, 2, 4, 6, 8, 10, 12, 20, 22, 24, 26, 28, 40, 74, 90, 112, 127, 129, 130, 146, 163, 191** by Paul I. Tanedo.

Page **iii** *left* Larry Downing/Reuters/Getty Images, *right* ©2001 *The Record* (Bergen County, NJ), Thomas E. Franklin, Staff Photographer/Corbis SABA; **35** Stone/Getty Images; **42** A.T.&T. Photo Center; **45** John Neubauer/PhotoEdit; **49** *left* Tony Freeman/PhotoEdit, *top right* Vic Bider/PhotoEdit, *bottom right* Michael Newman/PhotoEdit; **50** Irene Springer; **53** *top* Larry Fleming, *bottom left* Irene Springer, *bottom right* Stan Wakefield; **55** *top* NASA/Roger Ressmeyer/Corbis, *bottom left* Getty Images, *bottom right* ©2001 *The Record* (Bergen County, NJ), Thomas E. Franklin, Staff Photographer/Corbis SABA; **59** *top left* Cleve Bryant/PhotoEdit, *top middle* Cleve Bryant/PhotoEdit, *top right* Mark Wilson/Getty Images, *bottom left* Newsmakers/Getty Images, *bottom middle* AFP/Corbis, *bottom right* William Collins/Reuters/Getty Images; **60** Mark Anderson; **62** *top and middle* Courtesy of United Airlines, *bottom* Irene Springer; **64** UPI/Bettmann Newsphotos; **65** *left* AFP/Corbis, *right* William Collins/Reuters/Getty Images; **67** *left* Cleve Bryant/PhotoEdit, *middle* Cleve Bryant/PhotoEdit, *right* Mark Wilson/Getty Images; **71** *top left* Newsmakers/Getty Images, *top middle left* Mark Richards/PhotoEdit, *top middle right* Newsmakers/Getty Images, *top right* Newsmakers/Getty Images, *bottom left* AFP/Corbis, *bottom right* William Collins/Reuters/Getty Images; **72** Courtesy of United Airlines; **75** AFP/Corbis; **77** William Collins/Reuters/Getty Images; **80** Jonathan Nourok/PhotoEdit; **85** *top left* Getty Images, *bottom left* Irene Springer, *top middle* Newsmakers/Getty Images, *middle* Robert King/Newsmakers/Getty Images, *bottom middle* Rhoda Sidney/PhotoEdit, *top right* Eric Draper/Reuters/Getty Images, *middle right* Darren McCollester/Newsmakers/Getty Images, *bottom right* Reuters NewMedia Inc./Corbis; **86** Irene Springer; **88** John Spragens, Jr.; **89** *left* Stone/Getty Images, *center* S Bob Daemmrich/Stock Boston, *right* Karl Weatherly/Corbis; **91** *left* Arvind Garg, *middle* Arthur Glauberman, *right* Carl Scholfield; **92** National Archives; **93** Library of Congress; **99** *top left* Getty Images, *top right* Bettmann/Corbis, *bottom left* Getty Images, *bottom right* Bettmann/Corbis; **100** Getty Images; **103** *top and bottom* New York Public Library; **107** Bettmann/Corbis; **113** *top right* A. Ramey/PhotoEdit, *bottom left* Paul Conklin/PhotoEdit, *bottom right* Dave G. Houser/Corbis; **117** *top left* Getty Images, *top middle* Getty Images, *top right* Gary Conner/PhotoEdit, *bottom left* Getty Images, *bottom middle* Getty Images, *bottom right* Rudi Von Briel/PhotoEdit; **118** *left* Library of Congress, *right* A.T.&T. Photo Center; **120** National Archives; **122** Library of Congress; **124** Library of Congress; **126** *left* White House Collection, *right* National Archives; **128** *left* Irene Springer, *right* Florida Division of Tourism; **135** *top left* Rudi Von Briel/PhotoEdit, *top middle* A. Ramey/PhotoEdit, *top right* Stephen McBrady/PhotoEdit, *bottom left* Getty Images, *bottom middle* AFP/Corbis, *bottom left* Spencer Grant/PhotoEdit; **136** Library of Congress; **138** UPI/Bettmann Newsphotos; **139** *left* Marc Anderson, *right* Eric Draper/Reuters/Getty Images; **140** *top* UPI/Bettmann News Photos, *bottom left* Irene Springer, *bottom right* William Collins/Reuters/Getty Images; **143** National Archives; **144** Getty Images; **147** New York Public Library; **153** *top left* Library of Congress, *top right* Library of Congress, *bottom right* New York Public Library; **154** Library of Congress; **155** Larry Downing/Reuters/Getty Images; **158** *bottom* Valentine Museum, Richmond, Virginia; **159** *top left* Library of Congress, *top right* New York Historical Society, *bottom* Library of Congress; **160** Washington Convention and Visitors Bureau; **162** New York Public Library; **164** *left* AP/Wide World Photos, *right* Library of Congress; **171** *top left* Corbis, *top middle* Library of Congress, *top right* Robert Holmes/Corbis, *bottom left* Library of Congress, *bottom middle* Library of Congress, *bottom right* United Press International Photo; **172** *left* A.T.&T. Photo Center, *right* Levi Strauss and Company; **173** Library of Congress; **174** *top* Library of Congress, *middle* United Press International Photo, *bottom* Art West; **177** *top, middle and bottom* Library of Congress; **178** *top* National Archives, *bottom* U.S. Army Photograph; **179** *top* Robert Holmes/Corbis, *middle* United Press International Photo, *bottom* AP/Wide World Photos; **182** United Press International Photo; **184** *left* Automatic Voting Machine Division, Rockwell Manufacturing Company, *right* Marilyn Church; **185** *top and bottom* Library of Congress; **186** *top and bottom* Official Photograph, The White House, *middle* Library of Congress; **187** United National Photo by Yutaka Nagata; **188** *top* William Philport/Reuters/Getty Images, *bottom* Larry Downing/Reuters/Getty Images; **189** *left* Courtesy CNN, *right* Jeff Greenberg/PhotoEdit; **207** AFP/Corbis;

Cover www.comstock.com and Ed Pritchard/Stone/Getty Images.
Back cover *left and right* Reuters NewMedia Inc./Corbis.

Library of Congress Cataloging-in-Publication Data

Bliss, Bill.
    Voices of freedom: English and civics/Bill Bliss with Steven J. Molinsky.—3rd ed.
        p. cm.
    Includes index.
    ISBN 0-13-045266-1 (alk. paper)
        1. United States—Politics and government. 2. United States—History. I. Molinsky,
Steven J. II. Title.

JK1758.B585 2002   2002023576
320.473—dc21

ISBN: 0-13-045266-1

5 6 7 8 9 10–CRK–05 04

Oh, say, does that star-spangled banner yet wave
O'er the land of the free and the home of the brave.

—*Francis Scott Key*

CONTENTS

TO THE TEACHER vii

A Personal Information ★ Identification Cards ★ Numbers ★ Alphabet — 1

B Personal Information ★ Months of the Year ★ Dates — 19

1 Maps & Geography ★ Cities, States, & Capitals ★ Beliefs — 35

2 The Flag — 49

3 Branches of Government — 59

4 The Congress ★ The President ★ The Supreme Court — 71

5 Types of Government ★ State & Local Government ★ Public Officials ★ The Constitution ★ The Bill of Rights — 85

6 Discovery ★ Colonization — 99

7 The Revolutionary War ★ The Declaration of Independence — 117

8 The Constitution ★ Branches of Government ★ The Bill of Rights ★ George Washington — 135

9 The National Anthem ★ Expansion ★ The Civil War ★ Abraham Lincoln ★ Amendments — 153

10 Industrial Revolution ★ Labor Movement ★ Immigration ★ 20th-Century History ★ Civil Rights Movement ★ Citizens' Rights & Responsibilities ★ Presidents: 1961–Present ★ September 11, 2001 — 171

APPENDIX
100 Questions for Review — 199
Songs of Freedom — 204
Pledge of Allegiance — 207
Oath of Allegiance — 207
Scripts for Listening Exercises — 208
Sentences for Dictation Exercises — 210
Index — 212
Correlation Key — 214

To The Teacher

Voices of Freedom is a content-based English and Civics text for beginning-level learners of English. It offers students a basic introduction to U.S. history and government and features activities designed to promote civic participation. The text is designed to serve as a simple English/Civics social studies course for adult and secondary-school learners as well as a preparatory course for students who will be applying for citizenship.

The text covers basic government and history topics through a carefully controlled sequence of lessons that simultaneously teach beginning-level vocabulary and grammar. It is specifically designed for students whose limited language skills prevent them from using standard social studies or civics materials. This third edition includes many new features suggested by users of the previous editions:

- Vocabulary preview sections at the beginning of each chapter
- Civic participation activities and issue discussions designed to meet English/Civics program goals
- Expanded chapter tests to develop students' test-taking skills
- Project-based activities to promote active learning and student teamwork
- Internet activities that range from simple web-browsing to virtual field trips to important historical sites
- Chapter summaries highlighting key vocabulary and grammar

Students also have many opportunities to share information about the government and history of their native countries. In this way, *Voices of Freedom* aims to give respect and attention to each student's country, history, and culture as the student learns about the government, history, and civic life of the United States.

In addition to the civics curriculum, *Voices of Freedom* offers students critically important practice using functional interview skills—the communication strategies they will need if they are preparing for a naturalization

interview. The citizenship applicant's ability to handle the give-and-take of routine interview questions will often determine the examiner's assessment of English language ability. These strategies include Asking for Clarification; Asking for Repetition; Checking and Indicating Understanding; Correcting; Hesitating; and Reporting Personal Information.

INSTRUCTIONAL FORMATS AND ACTIVITIES

Voices of Freedom lessons provide the following types of activities:

Readings: Students are first introduced to basic information about government, history, and civics through short readings that are always accompanied by one or more photographs. The readings are designed for high readability by lowest-level students: they are printed in large-size type, each sentence appears on a separate line, and there is very generous spacing between lines and between paragraphs.

Interview Dialogs: These conversation practice activities provide students with authentic examples of the communication that occurs between an examiner and a citizenship applicant during a naturalization interview. These dialogs cover a wide range of topics, including personal identification, personal information about background and family, and question-and-answer exchanges about government, history, and civics. The interview dialogs provide crucial practice since an applicant's language ability will be assessed through the normal course of the interview.

Check-Up Exercises: These activities provide intensive skills practice in grammar, vocabulary, reading comprehension, and filling out forms. They essentially serve as a "workbook within the book" using standard exercise formats. To do these activities, students need little or no teacher instruction or supervision. The Check-Up Exercises are therefore very appropriate as homework.

"Questions & Answers" Activities: These unique lessons offer students critically important practice with the multiple ways a question might be posed by an examiner. Students first study various ways that a particular question might be worded, and then practice asking and answering questions with other students. In this way, students will not only know the answers, they will also "know the questions."

Listening Exercises: Each chapter offers students a listening activity, most of which require students to listen carefully for questions that sound the same or might otherwise be easily confused. Students are trained to listen closely to avoid mistakes they might make during an interview due to their misunderstanding of an examiner's question. For the teacher, scripts for the listening exercises appear at the back of the textbook and in the Teacher's Guide. All listening exercises are also included on the *Voices of Freedom* Audio Program.

Review Lessons: At the end of many chapters, students do one or more review exercises. These serve not only to review the content of the chapter but to cumulatively review content introduced earlier. Two unique formats for review activities are the "Information Exchange," in which students interview each other and record information collected during the interviews, and the "Talking Time Line," in which students match events with their dates, write the events on a time line, and then practice asking and answering questions based on the time line information.

Chapter Tests: Twenty-item multiple-choice tests at the end of each chapter evaluate student achievement of the chapter learning objectives while developing students' test-taking skills.

Dictation Exercises: At the end of each chapter test, students practice writing five sentences from dictation. This prepares them for the sentence-writing requirement during the citizenship examination. Scripts for the dictation exercises appear at the back of the book and in the Teacher's Guide.

Civics Enrichment Activities: New in the third edition, these activities at the end of each chapter promote students' active participation in class and in the civic life of the community.

Activities include:

CIVIC PARTICIPATION ACTIVITIES are designed to bring civics instruction alive by involving students in local government through visits to city hall and representatives' offices, attendance at local government or school board meetings, and classroom visits by local officials.

PROJECT ACTIVITIES enable students to work together in teams or as a class to decorate bulletin boards with civics content, create local maps, simulate an Election Day in class, or have a Thanksgiving celebration.

COMMUNITY ISSUES DISCUSSIONS encourage students to apply civics content to their own lives, to identify issues and problems related to their well-being in the community, and to brainstorm solutions.

DEBATES organize students into teams, each team taking one side of an issue and arguing positions in front of the class.

INTERNET ACTIVITIES use online resources to take virtual field trips to historic places, to visit the websites of government officials, and to do simple web-browsing tasks to find information.

100 Questions for Review: The text includes 100 common civics questions and answers arranged in a convenient double-column format, allowing students to use this section for practice as well as a self-check.

The Appendix: The appendix includes listening and dictation scripts, songs, the Oath of Allegiance that is recited at naturalization ceremonies, an index, and a correlation key that provides teachers with an easy resource for integrating the civics curriculum with lessons in the *Foundations*, *Side by Side*, *Word by Word*, and *ExpressWays* programs.

LOW BEGINNING-LEVEL STUDENTS

For students who are particularly low-level beginners, the first two preparatory chapters of *Voices of Freedom* have been designed to provide a solid, basic foundation in English communication and literacy. The chapters introduce the alphabet, numbers, and very basic vocabulary and expressions through the context of personal identification skills, in a format and a sequence that is appropriate for beginning-level students of English. The very easy exercise formats in these chapters, which involve circling, matching, and filling in boxes and blanks, are particularly designed to give low-level beginners a feeling of immediate success and momentum in their study of English and Civics. Students who already have some basic understanding of English can skip these preparatory chapters and begin their studies with Chapter One.

TEACHING TECHNIQUES

Voices of Freedom has been designed to be as easy-to-use as possible, for the teacher as well as the students. Exercise formats are simple and consistent so that students will need little or no explanation of how to complete the various activities.

Two of the central learning devices in the text are the readings and the interview dialogs. For these two types of activities, the following teaching steps are suggested. Teachers, however, should always feel free to use these activities in the way that is most appropriate for their teaching styles and their particular students.

Readings

1. Have students talk about the photograph and/or their own experiences in order to establish a context, or schema, for what they are about to read.
2. Have students read the story silently. (If you wish, you may read the story aloud or play the audio program as they read silently.)

3. Ask students a simple question about each line of the story. For low-level beginning students, ask the questions in the sequence of the story. For higher-level students, ask the questions out of sequence.
4. Ask students if they don't understand any vocabulary. Have students help define any unfamiliar words.
5. Do a choral repetition of the reading, line by line. (This is not reading practice, but is rather speaking practice. While such speaking practice is not usually done with a reading passage, it is appropriate in *Voices of Freedom* since each line of a reading is a possible answer to an examiner's question. This speaking practice prepares students for the interview dialog practice that will follow.)
6. Class Circle Reading. Have students read the passage as a class with different students reading each line in turn. You can assign who will read in a variety of ways: by seating patterns, by assigning each line of the passage, or by letting students take turns spontaneously.
7. Pair Practice. Have students work in pairs, reading the passage to each other paragraph by paragraph, for further speaking practice. Circulate around the room, checking students' reading and pronunciation, and focus more attention, if possible, on students who need more assistance.
8. When comprehension questions about the reading appear in the "Check-Up" exercises following a reading, have students first fill in their written answers, and then practice, in pairs, asking and answering these questions aloud.

Interview Dialogs

1. Set the scene. Have students look at the photograph and decide who the people are. You might simply mention in a word or two what they are talking about, such as "the flag" or "the Civil War."

2. Have students listen to the interview dialog with their books closed. Present the dialog yourself (taking both roles), present it with the help of another student, have two students present it to the rest of the class, or play the audio.

3. Choral Repetition. Have students repeat each line of the dialog in unison after you. (Books still closed.)

4. Have students open their books and look at the dialog. Ask if there are any questions about vocabulary.

5. Choral Conversation Practice.

   a. Divide the class into two groups (two halves or by rows). Have Group 1 say Speaker A's lines in unison, and have Group 2 say Speaker B's lines. Then reverse.

   and/or

   b. You say Speaker A's lines, and then the entire class says Speaker B's lines in unison. Then reverse.

6. Call on one or two pairs of students to present the dialog.

7. Pair Practice. Have students practice the dialog in pairs, taking turns being Speaker A and Speaker B. Encourage students to look at each other during the practice rather than "burying" their heads in the books. This will help their spoken language sound more authentic and conversational.

   (You can pair students in different ways. You can pair students of similar ability together and thereby focus your attention on those pairs of students who require more attention. Or you can pair weaker students with stronger ones so that your more-capable students have the opportunity to consolidate their skills while providing help to others in the class.)

Additional Communication Practice

Throughout *Voices of Freedom* there are many written exercises that include instructions to have students practice conversationally with another student. These include the "Questions and Answers" exercises, the "Information Exchange" activities, the "Talking Time Line" activities, and many of the review exercises. After students have completed the writing required for these exercises, whether at home or in class, they should practice asking and answering the questions aloud with another student. This additional speaking practice helps students consolidate their communication skills before moving on to the information to be presented in the succeeding lessons.

A FINAL WORD: THE "GOAL" OF CIVICS EDUCATION

At the beginning of the last century, the goal of citizenship education in so-called "Americanization" classes was to indoctrinate students with U.S. civics information in a way that often discredited their native countries and cultures. It was as though students had to renounce their backgrounds and heritages in order to acquire knowledge about their new country. In this new century, we aspire to a nobler effort: to offer students the language skills and civics knowledge they need to attain citizenship, to live full and productive lives, and to participate fully in the civic life of their communities and the country, and to do so through an educational program that recognizes and respects the diversity of cultures, histories, and experiences that our students bring to our classrooms . . . and the nation.

Bill Bliss

PERSONAL INFORMATION
IDENTIFICATION CARDS
ALPHABET
NUMBERS

- **To Be**
- **WH-Questions**

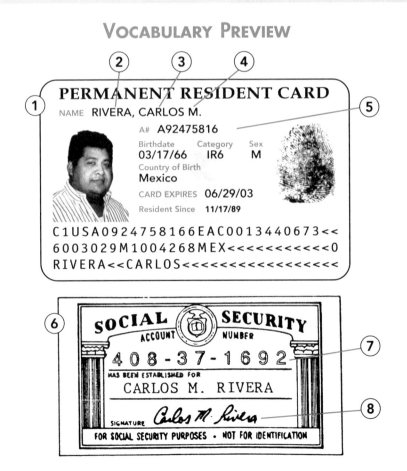

1. permanent resident card
2. last name / family name / surname
3. first name / given name
4. middle initial
5. "A"-number
6. social security card
7. social security number
8. signature

Applying for Citizenship

My name is Carlos Rivera.
My first name is Carlos.
My last name is Rivera.

I'm a permanent resident.
I'm applying for citizenship.
I want to be a citizen of the United States of America.

Check-Up

Circle the Same Word

1. name	first	(name)	last
2. My	I'm	is	My
3. last	last	name	first
4. citizen	name	first	citizen
5. first	name	last	name
6. permanent	permanent	citizen	resident

Vocabulary Check

permanent	applying	last	citizenship	name

1. My _____name_____ is Carlos Rivera.

2. I'm applying for _____.

3. My _____ name is Rivera.

4. I'm a _____ resident.

5. I'm _____ for citizenship.

How About You?

1. What's your first name? _____

2. What's your last name? _____

PERMANENT RESIDENT CARD

NAME   RIVERA, CARLOS M.

A# A92475816

Birthdate	Category	Sex
03/17/66	IR6	M

Country of Birth
Mexico

CARD EXPIRES 06/29/03

Resident Since   11/17/89

C1USA0924758166EAC0013440673<<
6003029M1004268MEX<<<<<<<<<<0
RIVERA<<CARLOS<<<<<<<<<<<<<<<<

I'm a permanent resident.
This is my permanent resident card.

My last name* is Rivera.
My first name† is Carlos.
My middle name is Manuel.
My full name is Carlos Manuel Rivera.

I'm applying for citizenship.
I want to be a citizen of the United States of America.

*last name = family name
            surname

† first name = given name

Grammar Check

a	want	my	I'm	is

1. My first name _____is_____ Carlos.

2. ___my___ middle name is Manuel.

3. I'm ___a___ permanent resident.

4. ___I'm___ applying for citizenship.

5. I ___want___ to be a citizen.

What's Your Name?

1. _____ _____ _____
   First Name   Middle Name   Last Name

2. _____ _____ _____
   Last Name   First Name   Middle Name

3. _____
   (Family Name) (Given Name) (Middle Name)

4. ☐☐☐☐☐☐☐☐☐☐ ☐☐☐☐☐☐☐☐ ☐☐☐☐☐☐☐☐
   Surname   First Name   Full Middle Name

Fill Out the Form

U.S. Department of Homeland Security
Bureau of Citizenship and Immigration Services

Print clearly or type your answers using CAPITAL letters.

Part 1. Your Name *(The Person Applying for Naturalization)*

A. Your current legal name.

Family Name *(Last Name)*

[   ]

Given Name *(First Name)*   Full Middle Name *(If applicable)*

[   ]   [   ]

Could You Spell That, Please?

The Alphabet

Aa Bb Cc Dd Ee Ff Gg Hh Ii Jj Kk Ll Mm
Nn Oo Pp Qq Rr Ss Tt Uu Vv Ww Xx Yy Zz

A. What's your family name?

B. Rivera.

A. Could you spell that, please?

B. R-I-V-E-R-A.

A. What's your first name?

B. Carlos.

A. And your middle name?

B. Manuel.

A. What's your family name?

B. _____.

A. Could you spell that, please?

B. _____.

A. What's your first name?

B. _____.

A. And your middle name?

B. _____.*

*Practice with another student, using the model dialog above as a guide.
Take turns asking and answering the questions.*

* If no middle name, say, "I don't have a middle name."

Alphabet Practice

Fill in the missing letters of the alphabet. Then use the letters to make a word.

1. [A] B C D [E] F G H I J K L [M][N] O P Q R S T U V W X Y Z
   [N][A][M][E]

2. [ ] B [ ][ ] E F G H I J K L M N O P Q [ ] S T U V W X Y Z
   [ ][ ][ ][ ]

3. [ ] B C D E F G H I J K [ ] M N O P Q R [ ][ ] U V W X Y Z
   [ ][ ][ ][ ]

4. [ ] B C D E [ ] G H [ ] J K [ ][ ] N O P Q R S T U V W X [ ] Z
   [ ][ ][ ][ ][ ][ ]

Listening

Listen and circle the correct answer.

1. (Martinez)   Rivera

2. Sanchez   Santos

3. Tran   Dang

4. Cruz   Ortiz

5. Long   Wong

Listen and write the name you hear.

1. _____ *Garcia* _____   4. _____

2. _____   5. _____

3. _____   6. _____

Numbers

0	zero
1	one
2	two
3	three
4	four
5	five
6	six
7	seven
8	eight
9	nine

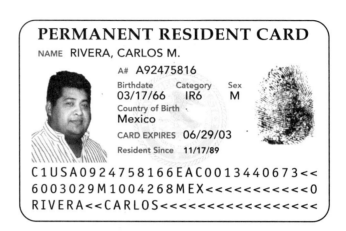

This is my permanent resident card.
My "A"-number is A-92475816.

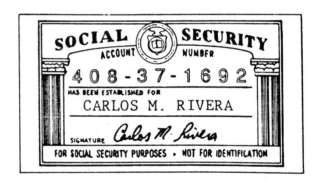

This is my social security card.
My social security number is 408-37-1692.*

RIVERA **Carlos M** 80 Stanley Av
     Los Angeles **213 257-9108**

This is my telephone number.
My telephone number is (213) 257-9108.

*0 = "zero" or "oh"

Check-Up

Matching

1. Name   A-92475816

2. Telephone Number   408-37-1692

3. Social Security Number   Carlos Rivera

4. "A"-Number   (213) 257-9108

Answer These Questions

1. What's your "A"-number?   A-__ __ __ __ __ __ __ __ __

2. What's your social security number?   __ __ __ -__ __ -__ __ __ __

3. What's your home telephone number? (Include area code)   (__ __ __) __ __ __ -__ __ __ __

4. What's your phone number at work? (Include area code)   (__ __ __) __ __ __ -__ __ __ __

Fill Out the Form

Write your "A"-number here:

A- __ __ __ __ __ __ __ __ __

Family Name (*Last Name*)

Given Name (*First Name*)

Full Middle Name (*If applicable*)

Daytime Phone Number (*If any*)

(   )

Evening Phone Number (*If any*)

(   )

Social Security Number

__ __ __ -__ __ -__ __ __ __

My Address

10 ten
11 eleven
12 twelve
13 thirteen
14 fourteen
15 fifteen
16 sixteen
17 seventeen
18 eighteen
19 nineteen
20 twenty
30 thirty
40 forty
50 fifty
60 sixty
70 seventy
80 eighty
90 ninety

My address is 80 Stanley Avenue.
My apartment number is 12-D.
The name of my city is Los Angeles.
The name of my state is California.
California is in the United States of America.
My zip code is 90048.

How About You?

My address is _____.

(My apartment number is _____.)

The name of my city is _____.

The name of my state is _____.

_____ is in the United States of America.

My zip code is _____.

Check-Up

Matching

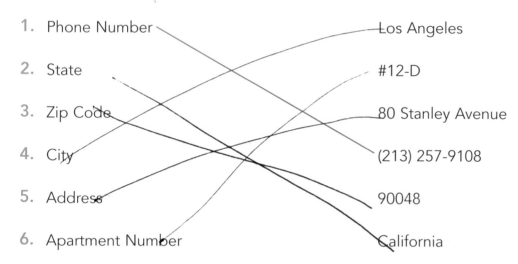

1. Phone Number
2. State
3. Zip Code
4. City
5. Address
6. Apartment Number

Los Angeles
#12-D
80 Stanley Avenue
(213) 257-9108
90048
California

Reading Addresses

80 Stanley Avenue	**eighty**
1628 Donaldson Street	**sixteen twenty-eight**
214 Conway Avenue	**two fourteen** / **two hundred and fourteen**

Say these addresses.

13 Stanley Avenue   4826 Greenwood Avenue
60 Spring Street   549 Parkman Avenue
1360 Donaldson Street   842 Main Street

Listening

Listen and circle the number you hear.

1. 60   (30)   4. 4256   4615

2. 13   19   5. 1839   3918

3. 15   50   6. 482   842

A. What's your file number?

B. You mean my "A"-number?

A. Yes.

B. It's A-92475816.

A. And what's your home telephone number including area code?

B. 213-257-9108.

A. And your work phone?*

B. 213-626-4377.

A. What's the name of your state?

B. California.

A. And your city?

B. Los Angeles.

A. What's your address?

B. 80 Stanley Avenue.

A. Apartment number?

B. 12-D.

A. Zip code?

B. 90048.

* work phone = phone number at work

A. What's your file number?

B. You mean my "A"-number?

A. Yes.

B. It's A-_____.

A. And what's your home telephone number including area code?

B. _____.

A. And your work phone?

B. _____.

A. What's the name of your state?

B. _____.

A. And your city?

B. _____.

A. What's your address?

B. _____.

A. Apartment number?

B. _____.*

A. Zip code?

B. _____.

Practice with another student, using the model dialog above as a guide. Take turns asking and answering the questions.

* If no apartment number, say "No."

Write Your Home Address

1. Home Address: _____
   Number   Street   Apt. No.

   _____
   City   State   Zip Code

2. Home Address: ☐☐☐☐☐☐☐☐☐☐☐☐☐☐☐☐☐☐☐☐☐☐☐☐
   Number   Street   Apt. No.

   ☐☐☐☐☐☐☐☐☐☐☐☐☐☐☐☐☐ ☐☐☐ ☐☐☐☐☐
   City   State   Zip Code

3. Home Address—Street Number and Name *(Do NOT write a P.O. Box in this space)*   Apartment Number

   City   County   State   ZIP Code   Country

Fill Out the Form

Family Name *(Last Name)*

Given Name *(First Name)*   Full Middle Name *(If applicable)*

Home Address–Street Number and Name *(Do NOT write a P.O.Box in this space)*   Apartment Number

City   County   State   ZIP Code   Country

Daytime Phone Number *(If any)*   Evening Phone Number *(If any)*   E-mail Address *(If any)*
(   )   (   )

Social Security Number
__ __ __ - __ - __ __ __ __

Write your "A"-number here:

A- __ __ __ __ __ __ __ __ __

⬅➡ Information Exchange

Read these questions and answer them.

> What's your family name?
> (Could you spell that, please?)
> What's your first name?
> What's your middle name?
> What's your home address?
> What's your apartment number?
> What's the name of your city?
> What's the name of your county?
> What's the name of your state?
> What's your zip code?
> What's your daytime telephone number including area code?
> What's your evening telephone number including area code?
> What's your social security number?
> What's your "A"-number?

Now use these questions to interview another student. Write the information below.

Family Name *(Last Name)*

[   ]

Given Name *(First Name)*   Full Middle Name *(If applicable)*

[   ]   [   ]

Home Address–Street Number and Name *(Do NOT write a P.O.Box in this space)*   Apartment Number

[   ]   [   ]

City   County   State   ZIP Code   Country

[   ]   [   ]   [   ]   [   ]   [   ]

Daytime Phone Number *(If any)*   Evening Phone Number *(If any)*

(   )   (   )

Social Security Number

__ __ __ - __ __ - __ __ __ __

Write your "A"-number here:

A- __ __ __ __ __ __ __ __

CHAPTER TEST

Choose the best answer.

Example:

My name is
- Ⓐ 14-C.
- Ⓑ 407-32-1289.
- ⬤ Hector Garcia.
- Ⓓ 10023.

A. PERSONAL INFORMATION

1. My social security number is
   - Ⓐ 75215.
   - Ⓑ (213) 735-1264.
   - Ⓒ A-95314726.
   - Ⓓ 407-32-7741.

2. My "A"-number is
   - Ⓐ 75215.
   - Ⓑ (213) 735-1264.
   - Ⓒ A-95314726.
   - Ⓓ 407-32-7741.

3. My zip code is
   - Ⓐ 75215.
   - Ⓑ (213) 735-1264.
   - Ⓒ A-95314726.
   - Ⓓ 407-32-7741.

4. My home telephone number is
   - Ⓐ 75215.
   - Ⓑ (213) 735-1264.
   - Ⓒ A-95314726.
   - Ⓓ 407-32-7741.

5. I'm a permanent
   - Ⓐ address.
   - Ⓑ card.
   - Ⓒ number.
   - Ⓓ resident.

6. The name of my state is
   - Ⓐ Los Angeles.
   - Ⓑ California.
   - Ⓒ the United States of America.
   - Ⓓ Carlos Rivera.

7. This is my social security
   - Ⓐ code.
   - Ⓑ phone.
   - Ⓒ card.
   - Ⓓ address.

8. My middle name is
   - Ⓐ Manuel.
   - Ⓑ Carlos Rivera.
   - Ⓒ 19-J.
   - Ⓓ surname.

9. What's your telephone
   - Ⓐ area?
   - Ⓑ number?
   - Ⓒ zip code?
   - Ⓓ address?

10. My address is
    - Ⓐ New York.
    - Ⓑ the United States of America.
    - Ⓒ 8-D.
    - Ⓓ 1642 Central Avenue.

11. I'm applying for
    - Ⓐ permanent.
    - Ⓑ zip code.
    - Ⓒ citizen.
    - Ⓓ citizenship.

12. What's your
    - Ⓐ spell that?
    - Ⓑ please?
    - Ⓒ family name?
    - Ⓓ at work?

B. VOCABULARY

13. My _____ name is Carlos Manuel Rivera.
    - Ⓐ first
    - Ⓑ last
    - Ⓒ middle
    - Ⓓ full

14. My _____ number is (213) 725-8319.
    - Ⓐ social security
    - Ⓑ telephone
    - Ⓒ "A"-
    - Ⓓ area code

15. The name of my _____ is Los Angeles.
    - Ⓐ city
    - Ⓑ state
    - Ⓒ zip code
    - Ⓓ address

16. My _____ is A-42731295.
    - Ⓐ area code
    - Ⓑ "A"-number
    - Ⓒ apartment number
    - Ⓓ social security number

17. My _____ is 42 Main Street.
    - Ⓐ city
    - Ⓑ state
    - Ⓒ zip code
    - Ⓓ address

18. My _____ is 10067.
    - Ⓐ city
    - Ⓑ state
    - Ⓒ zip code
    - Ⓓ address

19. My _____ number is 062-39-3728.
    - Ⓐ social security
    - Ⓑ telephone
    - Ⓒ "A"-
    - Ⓓ area code

20. I want to be a _____ of the United States of America.
    - Ⓐ family name
    - Ⓑ city
    - Ⓒ citizen
    - Ⓓ registration card

C. DICTATION

Listen and write.

1. _____

2. _____

3. _____

4. _____

5. _____

Civics Enrichment

Discuss: A permanent resident card and a social security card are forms of personal identification. What's another form of personal identification? Which do you have? Why are forms of personal identification important? Where do you get them?

Make a list of emergency telephone numbers for your community: Police, Fire, Ambulance, Poison Control Center. Make copies, and put a list next to each telephone where you live.

Discuss: Is it difficult to use emergency services in your community? Why?

CHAPTER SUMMARY

KEY VOCABULARY

PERSONAL INFORMATION

address
apartment
area code
avenue
city
country
county
family name
file number
first name
full name
given name
home
last name
middle name
name
number
phone
social security number
state
street
surname
telephone number
zip code

IDENTIFICATION CARDS

"A"-number
card
permanent resident card
social security card

IMMIGRATION STATUS

citizen
citizenship
permanent resident

FUNCTIONAL EXPRESSIONS

Could you spell that, please?
You mean . . . ?

OTHER WORDS

a
am
and
apply
capital letters
daytime
enter
evening
for
from
I
include
including
is
my
of
please
spell
that
the
this
United States of America
what
work
yes
your

NUMBERS

0	zero (oh)
1	one
2	two
3	three
4	four
5	five
6	six
7	seven
8	eight
9	nine
10	ten
11	eleven
12	twelve
13	thirteen
14	fourteen
15	fifteen
16	sixteen
17	seventeen
18	eighteen
19	nineteen
20	twenty
30	thirty
40	forty
50	fifty
60	sixty
70	seventy
80	eighty
90	ninety

GRAMMAR

TO BE

My name **is** Carlos Rivera.
I'm a permanent resident.

WH-QUESTIONS

What's your family name?

PERSONAL INFORMATION
MONTHS OF THE YEAR
DATES

- **To Be**
- **WH-Questions**
- **Yes/No Questions**
- **Short Answers**

VOCABULARY PREVIEW

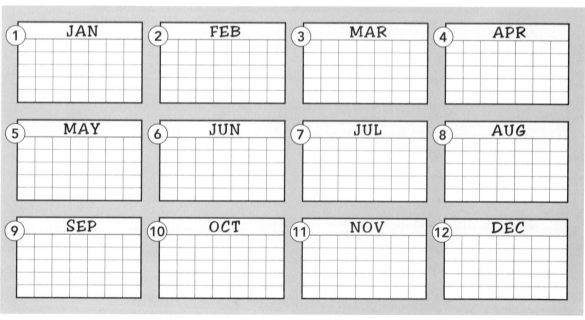

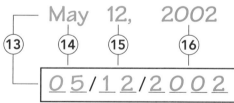

1.	January	5.	May	9.	September	13.	date
2.	February	6.	June	10.	October	14.	month
3.	March	7.	July	11.	November	15.	day
4.	April	8.	August	12.	December	16.	year

My name is Maria Lopez.
I'm from Mexico.
Now I'm a permanent resident of the United States.
The name of my city is Houston.
Houston is in the state of Texas.
Texas is a state in the United States.

I'm Mexican.
I was born in Monterrey.
Monterrey is in the state of Nuevo León.
Nuevo León is a state in Mexico.

I was born on May 4, 1972.
My mother's name is Gloria.
My father's name is Oscar.
My mother and father are in Monterrey.

I'm applying for naturalization.*
I want to be a citizen of the United States.

* naturalization = citizenship

Check-Up

Matching

1. My name is
2. I'm
3. I was born in
4. I was born on
5. I'm applying for

Monterrey.

naturalization.

Mexican.

Maria Lopez.

May 4, 1972.

Vocabulary Check

city	applying	born	name	mother	state

1. My _____ name _____ is Maria Lopez.

2. The name of my _____ is Houston.

3. The name of my _____ is Texas.

4. I was _____ in Monterrey.

5. My father and _____ are in Monterrey.

6. I'm _____ for citizenship.

Fill Out the Form

October 21, 1998	1 0 / 2 1 / 1 9 9 8
May 4, 1972	0 5 / 0 4 / 1 9 7 2

Date of Birth *(Month/Day/Year)*

__ __ / __ __ / __ __ __ __

Country of Birth

Sharing

Bring in photographs of people in your family. Tell about them.

This is my _____.

His/Her name is _____.

He/She is in _____.

(where?)

A. What's your place of birth?

B. Excuse me?

A. Where were you born? What's your native country?

B. I was born in Mexico.

A. In what city or town?

B. I was born in Monterrey.

A. Where is that?

B. Monterrey is in the state of Nuevo León.

A. What's your place of birth?

B. Excuse me?

A. Where were you born? What's your native country?

B. I was born in _____.

A. In what city or town?

B. I was born in _____.

A. Where is that?

B. _____ is in _____.

Practice with another student, using the model dialog above as a guide.
Take turns asking and answering the questions.

 **Check-Up**

Questions and Answers

Practice the different ways to ask these questions.

What's your nationality?	I'm **Mexican.**
What's your place of birth? What's your country of birth? What's your native country? What country are you from? Where were you born? Where are you from?	**Mexico.**
In what city or town were you born? What city or town were you born in? Where were you born?	I was born in **Monterrey.**

Now answer these questions.

1. What's your nationality? _____

2. What's your country of birth? _____

3. In what city or town were you born? _____

Grammar Check

Where   What

1. _____What_____ is your nationality?

2. _____ were you born?

3. _____ country are you from?

4. _____ city or town were you born in?

5. _____ are you from?

Map Activity

Bring in a map of your native country. Point to the city or town where you were born. Tell other students about that place.

A. What's your date of birth?

B. I'm sorry. I didn't understand. Could you please say that again?

A. When were you born?

B. I was born on May 4, 1972.

A. On May 4, 1972?

B. Yes. That's right.

A. What's your father's name?

B. Oscar Lopez.

A. And your mother's first name and maiden name?

B. Gloria Martinez.

A. What's your date of birth?

B. I'm sorry. I didn't understand. Could you please say that again?

A. When were you born?

B. I was born on _____.

A. On _____?

B. Yes. That's right.

A. What's your father's name?

B. _____.

A. And your mother's first name and maiden name?

B. _____.

Practice with another student, using the model dialog above as a guide.
Take turns asking and answering the questions.

Months and Years

Practice the months of the year.

January	April	July	October
February	May	August	November
March	June	September	December

Practice reading the years.

1972	nineteen seventy-two
1776	seventeen seventy-six
2001	two thousand one

Questions and Answers

Practice the different ways to ask these questions.

What year were you born?
In what year were you born?   I was born in **1972.**

In what month were you born?   I was born in **May.**

What's your date of birth?
What's your birth date?   I was born on **May 4, 1972.**
When were you born?

Now answer these questions.

1. What year were you born? _____

2. In what month were you born? _____

3. What's your date of birth? _____

Calendar Activity

Bring in a calendar that you can write on. Ask other students, "When were you born?"
Write their birthdays on the calendar. Then, discuss other important dates, such as U.S.
holidays and native country holidays, and add these to the calendar.

A. Are you still living at 86 Central Avenue?

B. Yes, I am.

A. And is your zip code 10715?

B. Yes, it is.

A. Are you still living at 65 Main Street?

B. No, I'm not.

A. 65 Main Street isn't your current address?

B. No, it isn't. My new address is 1247 Washington Street in Arlington.

A. And what's the zip code?

B. 22215.

A. Are you still living at _____?

B. Yes, I am.

A. And is your zip code _____?

B. Yes, it is.

A. Are you still living at _____?

B. No, I'm not.

A. _____ isn't your current address?

B. No, it isn't. My new address is _____

in _____.

A. And what's the zip code?

B. _____.

Choose the dialog that fits your situation and practice with another student.
Take turns asking and answering the questions.

 **Check-Up**

Grammar Check

| I am | I'm not | it is | it isn't |

1. Are you still living at 45 Park Street?

   Yes, _____ I am _____.

2. Is your zip code 10019?

   Yes, _____.

3. Are you from Guatemala?

   No, _____.

4. Is 1896 Central Avenue your current address?

   No, _____.

Let Me Verify Some Information

A. Let me verify some information. Your family name is Garcia.
Is that right?

B. Yes, it is.

A. And your first name is Victor. Is that correct?

B. No, it isn't. My first name is Francisco. My MIDDLE name is Victor.

A. I see. Your nationality is Mexican?

B. Yes. That's right.

A. Born in Guadalajara?

B. Yes. That's correct.

A. And is your date of birth November 20, 1968?

B. No. That's not correct. My date of birth is OCTOBER 20, 1968.

A. All right. What's your social security number?

B. 412-73-9648.

A. And on what date did you become a permanent resident?

B. On April 10, 1990.

A. Let me verify some information. Your family name is

_____. Is that right?

B. Yes, it is.

A. And your first name is _____. Is that correct?

B. No, it isn't. My first name is _____. My MIDDLE

name is _____.

A. I see. Your nationality is _____?

B. Yes. That's right.

A. Born in _____?

B. Yes. That's correct.

A. And is your date of birth _____?

B. No. That's not correct. My date of birth is _____.

A. All right. What's your social security number?

B. _____.

A. And on what date did you become a permanent resident?

B. On _____.

Practice with another student, using the model dialog above as a guide.
Take turns asking and answering the questions.

Fill Out the Form

Part 3. Information About You	Write your "A"-number here:
	A- __ __ __ __ __ __ __ __ __

A. Social Security Number
__ __ __-__ __-__ __ __ __

B. Date of Birth *(Month/Day/Year)*
__ __ / __ __ / __ __ __ __

C. Date You Became a Permanent Resident *(Month/Day/Year)*
__ __ / __ __ / __ __ __ __

D. Country of Birth

E. Country of Nationality

F. Are either of your parents U.S. citizens? *(If yes, see instructions)* ☐ Yes ☐ No

Check-Up

Questions and Answers

Practice the different ways to ask and answer these questions.

Is your family name Garcia?
Your family name is Garcia. Is that right?
Your family name is Garcia. Is that correct?
Your family name is Garcia?

Yes.	No.
Yes, **it is**.	No, **it isn't**.
Yes. That's correct.	No. That's not correct.
Yes. That's right.	No. That's not right.

Now answer these questions.

1. Your native country is Mexico.
   Is that right?   _____

2. Your telephone number is 241-6289.   _____
   Is that correct?

3. Is your home in Los Angeles?   _____

Listening

*On Line **A**, write your **place** of birth. On Line **B**, write your **date** of birth.*

A. _____	B. _____

*Now listen and circle **A** or **B**.*

1. (A)   B   4. A   B

2. A   B   5. A   B

3. A   B   6. A   B

 **Information Exchange**

Read these questions and answer them.

> What's your name?
> (Could you spell that, please?)
> What's your nationality?
> What country are you from?
> In what city or town were you born?
> What's your date of birth?

Now use these questions to interview other students. Write the information below.

	Name	Nationality	Country	City or Town	Date of Birth
1.					
2.					
3.					
4.					
5.					
6.					

Additional Practice

Ask and answer these questions. Practice with other students.

1. What's the name of your state?
2. What's the name of your city?
3. What's your home address?
4. What's your zip code?
5. What's your home telephone number including area code?
6. What's your work phone number including area code?
7. What's your nationality?
8. What's your country of birth?
9. In what city or town were you born?

CHAPTER TEST

Choose the best answer.

Example:

My zip code is
- (A) 93.
- (B) Florida.
- (●) 60018.
- (D) 412-33-7956.

A. PERSONAL INFORMATION

1. I was born on
   - (A) my native country.
   - (B) November 3, 1967.
   - (C) Mexico City.
   - (D) California.

2. 394 Main Street is my current
   - (A) zip code.
   - (B) address.
   - (C) phone number.
   - (D) social security number.

3. My date of birth is
   - (A) 1971.
   - (B) 276-8754.
   - (C) 11/14/1973.
   - (D) 90047.

4. My social security number is
   - (A) 421-36-9862.
   - (B) 553-1429.
   - (C) (212) 553-1429.
   - (D) 22148.

5. My zip code is
   - (A) 2001.
   - (B) 276-9802.
   - (C) 10/22/1999.
   - (D) 90047.

6. My home telephone number including area code is
   - (A) 421-36-9862.
   - (B) 553-1429.
   - (C) (212) 553-1429.
   - (D) 22148.

7. Guatemala is my native
   - (A) birth.
   - (B) nationality.
   - (C) date.
   - (D) country.

8. Houston is in the state of
   - (A) Texas.
   - (B) the United States.
   - (C) Los Angeles.
   - (D) Mexico.

9. My nationality is
   - (A) Texas.
   - (B) the United States.
   - (C) Mexico.
   - (D) Mexican.

10. My country of birth is
    - (A) Monterrey.
    - (B) Texas.
    - (C) Mexico.
    - (D) Nuevo León.

11. I'm a permanent
    - (A) city.
    - (B) nationality.
    - (C) resident.
    - (D) citizen.

12. Where were you
    - (A) birth?
    - (B) born?
    - (C) place of birth?
    - (D) native country?

B. VOCABULARY

13. The name of my _____ is Texas.
    - (A) state
    - (B) city
    - (C) country
    - (D) place

14. My _____ is 12 Main Street.
    - (A) country
    - (B) current address
    - (C) date of birth
    - (D) town

15. My _____ maiden name is Martinez.
    - (A) city's
    - (B) state's
    - (C) father's
    - (D) mother's

16. My _____ of birth is November 12, 1981.
    - (A) date
    - (B) country
    - (C) place
    - (D) nationality

17. I was born on _____ 14, 1979.
    - (A) Marco
    - (B) Maria
    - (C) March
    - (D) Mary

18. What's your _____ birth?
    - (A) city or town
    - (B) were
    - (C) where
    - (D) place of

19. Could you please _____ that again?
    - (A) understand
    - (B) right
    - (C) say
    - (D) sorry

20. Yes. That's _____.
    - (A) current
    - (B) correct
    - (C) is
    - (D) it is

C. DICTATION

Listen and write.

1. _____

2. _____

3. _____

4. _____

5. _____

Civics Enrichment

As a class, go around your school and introduce yourselves to the people in the office, the library, or other places. Tell your name, your nationality, where you were born, when you came to the United States, and other information.

Bulletin Board Project: Bring in a real map of your native country, or draw a map. Write a paragraph about yourself. Tell your name, your nationality, your country of birth, and the city or town where you were born. As a class, make a bulletin board display of student maps and paragraphs. Use string to connect students' places of birth on the maps to the paragraphs.

Calendar Project: As a class, make a calendar of all the months you will study together. On the calendar, write student birthdays, U.S. holidays, native country holidays, and other special dates. Hang the calendar on a wall or bulletin board.

CHAPTER SUMMARY

KEY VOCABULARY

PERSONAL INFORMATION

address	information
area code	maiden name
birth	middle name
birth date	name
born	nationality
city	native country
country	place of birth
country of birth	social security
country of	number
nationality	state
current address	street
date	telephone
date of birth	number
family name	town
first name	work phone
home address	number
home telephone	zip code
number	

FAMILY MEMBERS

father
mother
parents

TIME EXPRESSIONS

date
day
month
year

IMMIGRATION STATUS

citizen
citizenship
naturalization
permanent
    resident
U.S. citizen

MONTHS

January
February
March
April
May
June
July
August
September
October
November
December

FUNCTIONAL EXPRESSIONS

All right.
Could you please say
    that again?
Excuse me.
I didn't understand.
I'm sorry.
Is that correct?
Is that right?
Let me . . .
That's right.
That's correct.
That's not correct.

GRAMMAR

TO BE

My name **is** Maria Lopez.
I**'m** from Mexico.
My mother and father **are**
    in Monterrey.

WH-QUESTIONS

What's your place of birth?
Where were you born?
When were you born?

YES/NO QUESTIONS

Are you still living at 86 Central Avenue?
Is your zip code 10715?

SHORT ANSWERS

Yes, I am.
No, I'm not.

Yes, it is.
No, it isn't.

MAPS & GEOGRAPHY
CITIES, STATES, & CAPITALS
BELIEFS

- **Simple Present Tense**
- **Simple Present Tense vs. To Be**
- **WH-Questions**
- **Yes/No Questions**
- **Short Answers**

VOCABULARY PREVIEW

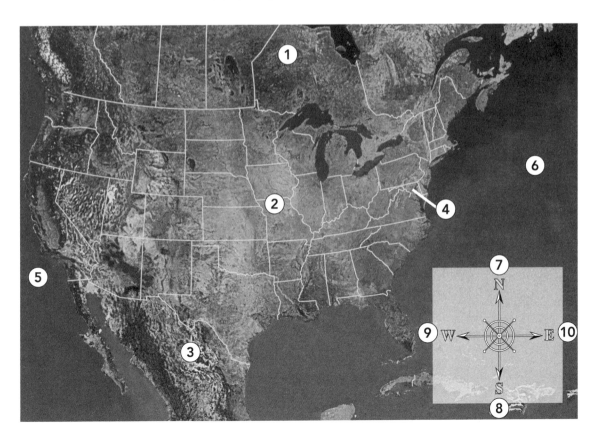

1. Canada
2. the United States
3. Mexico
4. Washington, D.C.
5. Pacific Ocean
6. Atlantic Ocean
7. north
8. south
9. west
10. east

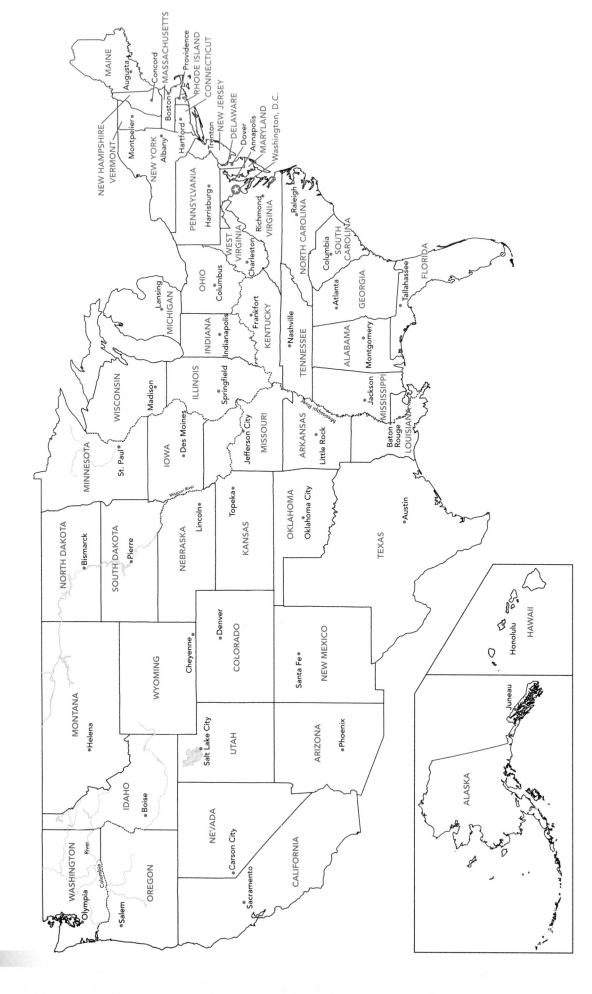

This is a map of our country.
It's a map of the United States of America.

The United States is a large country.
The United States is between two other countries.
Canada is north of the United States.
Mexico is south of the United States.

The United States is between two oceans.
The Atlantic Ocean is east of the United States.
The Pacific Ocean is west of the United States.

The capital of the United States is Washington, D.C.

What's the name of your state?
Point to your state on the map.

What's the name of your state capital?
Point to your state capital on the map.

What's the name of the capital of the United States?
Point to the capital of the United States on the map.

Map Discussion

Where did you first enter the United States?
Do you have any friends or family members in other states? Where?
Which states do you want to visit? Why?

Check-Up

Vocabulary Check

north	south	east	west	capital	country

1. The United States is a large _____*country*_____.

2. Canada is _____ of the United States.

3. The _____ of the United States is Washington, D.C.

4. The Atlantic Ocean is _____ of the United States.

5. The Pacific Ocean is _____ of the United States.

6. Mexico is _____ of the United States.

Grammar Check

Yes, it is.	No, it isn't.

1. Is the United States a large country? _____*Yes, it is.*_____

2. Is the capital of the United States in California? _____

3. Is Canada north of the United States? _____

4. Is the Atlantic Ocean west of the United States? _____

5. Is the United States between Canada and Mexico? _____

6. Is Washington, D.C. the capital of the United States? _____

Map Game

Think of a state and have other students guess it. Give them clues, using the words north, south, east, and west. Give clues one at a time until the students guess correctly. For example: "I'm thinking of a state that's east of Arizona," "It's west of Louisiana," and so on.

Your Native Country

Draw a map of your native country. On the map, show the capital, show your city or town, and show what is north, south, east, and west of your native country.

Now answer these questions.

1. What's the name of your native country?

   _____

2. What's the capital of your native country?

   _____

3. What city or town are you from?

   _____

4. What is north of your native country? south? east? west?

   _____

   _____

   _____

   _____

   _____

A. What state do you live in?

B. I live in Texas.

A. What city do you live in?

B. I live in Dallas.

A. Name the capital of the United States.

B. Washington, D.C.

A. And name the capital of your state.

B. Austin.

A. What state do you live in?

B. I live in _____.

A. What city do you live in?

B. I live in _____.

A. Name the capital of the United States.

B. Washington, D.C.

A. And name the capital of your state.

B. _____.

*Practice with another student, using the model dialog above as a guide.
Take turns asking and answering the questions.*

 **Check-Up**

Questions and Answers

Practice the different ways to ask these questions. Then write the answers.

1. What's the name of your state?
    What state do you live in? _____

2. What's the name of your city?
    What city do you live in? _____

What's the name of _____? = Name _____.

---

3. What's the name of the capital of the United States?
    What's the capital of the United States?
    Name the capital of the United States.

    _____

4. What's the name of the capital of your state?
    What's the capital of your state?
    Name the capital of your state.

    _____

Listening

*On Line **A**, write the name of your state.*
*On Line **B**, write the name of your state capital.*
*On Line **C**, write the name of the capital of the United States.*

A. _____ B. _____ C. _____

*Now listen and circle **A**, **B**, or **C**.*

1. A   B   C   4. A   B   C

2. A   B   C   5. A   B   C

3. A   B   C   6. A   B   C

I Believe in the United States

My name is Stanislaw Bienkowski.
I live in Chicago.
Chicago is a big city in Illinois.

I believe in the United States.
I believe in the United States government.
I believe in the United States Constitution.
I don't believe in Communism.

I am not a member of the Communist Party.
I am not a member of any other totalitarian party.
I am not a member of any terrorist organization.

I believe in freedom and democracy.
I'm applying for naturalization.
I want to be a citizen of the United States.

Check-Up

Did You Understand?

Answer these questions based on the story.

1. What's his name? _____

2. Where does he live? _____

3. Does he believe in Communism? _____

4. What does he believe in? _____

5. What does he want to be? _____

Vocabulary Check

| citizen | state | democracy | naturalization | city | capital |

1. Chicago is a large _____ *city* _____.

2. I believe in _____.

3. I want to be a _____ of the United States.

4. I'm applying for _____.

5. Washington, D.C. is the _____ of the United States.

6. Illinois is a _____ in the United States.

Discussion

What do the words *freedom* and *democracy* mean to you?
Do people in your native country have freedom and democracy? Explain.
Do all people in the United States have freedom and democracy? Explain.

Grammar Check

Yes, I do.	No, I don't.

1. Do you believe in the United States?   _____ *Yes, I do.* _____

2. Do you believe in Communism? _____

3. Do you believe in the United States Constitution? _____

4. Do you want to be a citizen of the United States some day? _____

5. Do you live in Chicago? _____

6. Do you believe in the United States government? _____

Yes, I am.	Yes, I do.
No, I'm not.	No, I don't.

7. Are you a permanent resident? _____

8. Are you a citizen of the United States? _____

9. Do you live in Washington, D.C.? _____

10. Are you a member of the Communist Party? _____

11. Do you believe in the United States government? _____

12. Are you applying for naturalization? _____

 # Review

Ask and answer these questions. Practice with other students.

1. What's your name?
2. Where are you from?
3. What state do you live in?
4. What city do you live in?
5. Name the capital of your state.
6. Name the capital of the United States.
7. Do you believe in Communism?
8. Do you believe in the United States Constitution?
9. Do you want to be a citizen of the United States some day?

America the Beautiful

O beautiful for spacious skies,
for amber waves of grain,
For purple mountain majesties,
above the fruited plain!
America! America!
God shed His grace on thee,
And crown thy good with brotherhood,
from sea to shining sea.

—*Katharine Lee Bates*

Katharine Lee Bates wrote her poem America the Beautiful *in 1893 after a visit to Pike's Peak, a 14,110-foot mountain in Colorado. The music for this famous song is by Samuel Augustus Ward.*

CHAPTER TEST

Choose the best answer.

Example:

Los Angeles is a large
- Ⓐ country.
- ● city.
- ⓒ state.
- Ⓓ ocean.

A. CITIES, STATES, CAPITALS, & GEOGRAPHY

1. The United States is a large
   - Ⓐ state.
   - Ⓑ ocean.
   - ⓒ country.
   - Ⓓ city.

2. The capital of the United States is
   - Ⓐ Austin.
   - Ⓑ Sacramento.
   - ⓒ Albany.
   - Ⓓ Washington, D.C.

3. Canada is
   - Ⓐ north of the United States.
   - Ⓑ south of the United States.
   - ⓒ east of the United States.
   - Ⓓ west of the United States.

4. Mexico is
   - Ⓐ north of the United States.
   - Ⓑ south of the United States.
   - ⓒ east of the United States.
   - Ⓓ west of the United States.

5. The United States is between two
   - Ⓐ states.
   - Ⓑ cities.
   - ⓒ maps.
   - Ⓓ oceans.

6. The Pacific Ocean is
   - Ⓐ north of the United States.
   - Ⓑ south of the United States.
   - ⓒ east of the United States.
   - Ⓓ west of the United States.

7. The Atlantic Ocean is
   - Ⓐ north of the United States.
   - Ⓑ south of the United States.
   - ⓒ east of the United States.
   - Ⓓ west of the United States.

8. Texas is a large
   - Ⓐ street.
   - Ⓑ capital.
   - ⓒ city.
   - Ⓓ state.

9. Sacramento is the capital of
   - Ⓐ North Carolina.
   - Ⓑ California.
   - ⓒ Texas.
   - Ⓓ Florida.

10. The capital of Florida is
    - Ⓐ Albany.
    - Ⓑ Atlanta.
    - ⓒ Tennessee.
    - Ⓓ Tallahassee.

11. Texas is east of
    - Ⓐ California.
    - Ⓑ New Jersey.
    - ⓒ Florida.
    - Ⓓ New York.

12. Illinois is west of
    - Ⓐ New Mexico.
    - Ⓑ Oregon.
    - ⓒ Pennsylvania.
    - Ⓓ Nevada.

B. GRAMMAR & VOCABULARY

13. I _____ believe in Communism.
- Ⓐ is not
- Ⓑ am not
- Ⓒ doesn't
- Ⓓ don't

14. I want to be a United States _____.
- Ⓐ capital
- Ⓑ citizen
- Ⓒ city
- Ⓓ government

15. I _____ in freedom and democracy.
- Ⓐ want
- Ⓑ want to
- Ⓒ believe
- Ⓓ believes

16. I _____ a member of the Communist Party.
- Ⓐ is not
- Ⓑ are not
- Ⓒ am not
- Ⓓ don't

17. My father _____ in Chicago.
- Ⓐ live
- Ⓑ lives
- Ⓒ believe
- Ⓓ want

18. Do you believe in the United States?
- Ⓐ Yes, I do.
- Ⓑ Yes, I am.
- Ⓒ Yes, he does.
- Ⓓ Yes, you are.

19. Are you a citizen?
- Ⓐ No, I don't.
- Ⓑ No, you don't.
- Ⓒ No, I'm not.
- Ⓓ No, he doesn't.

20. _____ you believe in freedom and democracy?
- Ⓐ Do
- Ⓑ Does
- Ⓒ Are
- Ⓓ Am

C. DICTATION

Listen and write.

1. _____

2. _____

3. _____

4. _____

5. _____

Civics Enrichment

Look at a local street map of your community. What kind of information do you see on the map? Find your school on the map. Find where you and other students live. Look for other kinds of maps of your community (such as a bus route map, a subway map, a map of parks, a map for bicycle riders). Bring the maps to class. Discuss what kinds of information you see on the maps.

Make a big tourist map for visitors to your community! On your map, draw all the important places to visit and show where they are. Try to show all the important streets. Also show any bus or train routes tourists can use to visit the places on your map.

Discuss with other students: Is your neighborhood in a good location or a bad location? Is your school in a good location or a bad location? Is it difficult to get from your neighborhood to your school? Is it difficult to get from your neighborhood to other important places in your community? What kind of transportation is there in your community? Do students have any problems with transportation?

CHAPTER SUMMARY

KEY VOCABULARY

GEOGRAPHY

Atlantic Ocean	Mexico
Austin	ocean
Canada	Pacific Ocean
capital	state
Chicago	state capital
city	Texas
country	town
Dallas	the United States
Illinois	of America
map	Washington, D.C.

COMPASS DIRECTIONS

east
north
south
west

PERSONAL INFORMATION

family members
name
native country

OTHER VOCABULARY

apply	member
believe	name (v.)
between	naturalization
big	other
citizen	party
Communism	permanent resident
Communist Party	point
Constitution	some day
democracy	terrorist organization
enter	totalitarian
freedom	visit
friends	want to
government	what
large	where
live	which

GRAMMAR

TO BE

The United States **is** a large country.
I **am not** a member of the Communist Party.

SIMPLE PRESENT TENSE

I **live** in Texas.
I **don't believe** in Communism.

WH-QUESTIONS

What's the name of your state?
Where does he live?

YES/NO QUESTIONS

Is the United States a large country?
Are you a permanent resident?
Do you believe in the United States?

SHORT ANSWERS

Yes, it is.
No, it isn't.

Yes, I am.
No, I'm not.

Yes, I do.
No, I don't.

THE FLAG

- ## There Is / There Are
- ## Singular / Plural
- ## Have / Has

VOCABULARY PREVIEW

1. flag
2. flagpole

3. stars
4. stripes

5. Pledge of Allegiance

The Flag of the United States

There are three colors on the flag of the United States.
The flag is red, white, and blue.

There are fifty states in the United States.
There are fifty stars on the American flag.
There is one star for each state.

There are thirteen stripes on the American flag.
The stripes are red and white.
There are seven red stripes and six white stripes.
There is one stripe for each of the first thirteen states
    in the United States.
The first thirteen states were called colonies.

 **Check-Up**

Did You Understand?

Answer these questions based on the story. Use full sentences.

1. What are the colors of the American flag?

   _____

2. How many states are there in the United States?

   _____

3. How many stars are there on the American flag?

   _____

4. How many stripes are there on the flag?

   _____

5. What colors are the stripes?

   _____

Vocabulary Check

stripes	red	colors	colonies	blue	stars

1. The American flag is red, white, and _____ blue _____ .

2. There are thirteen _____ on the American flag.

3. There are fifty _____ on the American flag.

4. There are three _____ on the flag of the United States.

5. The stripes on the flag are _____ and white.

6. The first thirteen states were called _____ .

Grammar Check

There is	There are

1. _____There are_____ fifty states in the United States.

2. _____ one star for each state.

3. _____ fifty stars on the American flag.

4. _____ thirteen stripes on the flag.

5. _____ one stripe for each of the first thirteen colonies.

6. _____ seven red stripes and six white stripes.

Your Native Country's Flag

Draw the flag of your native country.

Now answer the questions.

1. How many colors are there on your native country's flag?

   _____

2. What are the colors of the flag?

   _____

3. Describe the flag. What's on it?

   _____

   _____

A. How many stars does the American flag have?

B. I'm sorry. Could you please repeat the question?

A. Certainly. How many stars does the American flag have?

B. Uh . . . let me see. It has fifty stars.

A. That's right.

A. How many _____ does the American flag have?

B. I'm sorry. Could you please repeat the question?

A. Certainly. How many _____ does the American flag have?

B. Uh . . . let me see. It has _____ _____.

A. That's right.

Practice these exercises with another student, using the model dialog above as a guide. Take turns asking and answering the questions.

1. stripes
   thirteen

2. colors
   three

Check-Up

Questions and Answers

Practice the different ways to ask and answer these questions.

How many colors are there on the American flag?	=	How many colors does the American flag have?
There are three colors on the American flag.	=	The American flag has three colors.

Now answer these questions using full sentences.

1. How many stripes does the American flag have?

   _____

2. How many stripes are there on the American flag?

   _____

3. How many stars does the American flag have?

   _____

4. How many states are there in the United States?

   _____

Listening

Listen and circle the correct answer.

1.
   50
   13

2.
   50
   13

3.
   13
   3

4.
   stripes
   colonies

5.
   red and white
   red, white, and blue

6.
   red and white
   red, white, and blue

The Pledge of Allegiance

I pledge allegiance
to the flag
of the United States of America,
and to the republic
for which it stands,
one nation,
under God,
indivisible,
with liberty
and justice
for all.

Astronauts Neil Armstrong and Buzz Aldrin plant the U.S. flag on the moon on July 20, 1969.

U.S. Marines raise the U.S. flag at the top of Mount Suribachi, a mountain on the island of Iwo Jima, during a World War II battle on February 23, 1945.

Firefighters raise the American flag at the site of the World Trade Center in New York City after the terrorist attack on September 11, 2001.

CHAPTER TEST

Choose the best answer.

Example:

The flag of the United States has

Ⓐ two colors.

● three colors.

Ⓒ thirteen colors.

Ⓓ fifty colors.

A. THE FLAG

1. The colors of the American flag are
   Ⓐ red and white.
   Ⓑ red and blue.
   Ⓒ red, white, and brown.
   Ⓓ red, white, and blue.

2. The American flag has
   Ⓐ two stripes.
   Ⓑ three stripes.
   Ⓒ thirteen stripes.
   Ⓓ fifty stripes.

3. The flag of the United States has
   Ⓐ three stars.
   Ⓑ thirteen stars.
   Ⓒ fifty stars.
   Ⓓ one hundred stars.

4. The American flag has thirteen
   Ⓐ stripes.
   Ⓑ stars.
   Ⓒ colors.
   Ⓓ states.

5. The American flag has one star for each
   Ⓐ city.
   Ⓑ state.
   Ⓒ citizen.
   Ⓓ colony.

6. There is one stripe on the U.S. flag for each of the first
   Ⓐ three states.
   Ⓑ seven states.
   Ⓒ thirteen states.
   Ⓓ fifty states.

7. The U.S. flag has
   Ⓐ red and blue stars.
   Ⓑ red and blue stripes.
   Ⓒ red and white stars.
   Ⓓ red and white stripes.

8. The stripes on the U.S. flag are
   Ⓐ red.
   Ⓑ white.
   Ⓒ red and blue.
   Ⓓ white and red.

9. There are fifty states
   Ⓐ on the stars and stripes.
   Ⓑ in the United States.
   Ⓒ in the American colonies.
   Ⓓ on the American flag.

10. There are three
    Ⓐ stripes on the U.S. flag.
    Ⓑ stars on the U.S. flag.
    Ⓒ colors on the U.S. flag.
    Ⓓ states on the U.S. flag.

11. The first thirteen states were called
    Ⓐ capitals.
    Ⓑ colonies.
    Ⓒ countries.
    Ⓓ citizens.

12. Which color ISN'T on the flag of the United States?
    Ⓐ Blue.
    Ⓑ Brown.
    Ⓒ Red.
    Ⓓ White.

B. GRAMMAR & VOCABULARY

13. There are fifty _____ in the United States.
    - (A) stars
    - (B) stripes
    - (C) states
    - (D) flags

14. There are fifty _____ on the American flag.
    - (A) stars
    - (B) stripes
    - (C) states
    - (D) colors

15. There are _____ colors on the U.S. flag.
    - (A) three
    - (B) thirteen
    - (C) fifteen
    - (D) fifty

16. _____ one star on the American flag for each state.
    - (A) There are
    - (B) There is
    - (C) There
    - (D) Is

17. _____ three colors on the U.S. flag.
    - (A) There
    - (B) There is
    - (C) There are
    - (D) How many

18. The flag _____ stars and stripes.
    - (A) are
    - (B) there are
    - (C) have
    - (D) has

19. How many stripes _____ on the flag?
    - (A) is there
    - (B) are there
    - (C) has
    - (D) have

20. How many stars does the American flag _____?
    - (A) is there
    - (B) are there
    - (C) has
    - (D) have

C. DICTATION

Listen and write.

1. _____

2. _____

3. _____

4. _____

5. _____

Civics Enrichment

Discuss: Where do you see the flag of the United States in your community? What other flags do you see? What's on the flag of your state? What are the colors of your state flag?

Bulletin Board "Flags of the World" Project: On a large piece of paper, draw a color picture of the flag of your native country. Write some sentences about the flag. As a class, make a bulletin board display of all the flags and information. (You can also put photographs and names of students next to their flags.)

Internet Research: Go to www.yahoo.com or another search engine on the Internet. Type in the keywords "American flag". Look for information to answer these questions: When does the flag fly at *half-mast* (in the middle of the flagpole, not at the top)? If you want to fly the flag at night, what must you do? When does the flag fly in front of the White House in Washington, D.C.?

CHAPTER SUMMARY

KEY VOCABULARY

THE FLAG
American flag
flag
star
stripe
U.S. flag

COLORS
blue
brown
red
white

PLACES
island
Iwo Jima
moon
mountain
Mount Suribachi
United States
World Trade Center

PEOPLE
astronaut
firefighter
U.S. Marines

EVENTS
battle
terrorist attack
World War II

OTHER WORDS
colonies
native country
plant (v.)
raise (v.)
site
states
top

FUNCTIONAL EXPRESSIONS
Certainly.
Could you please repeat
  the question?
That's right.
Uh . . . let me see.

GRAMMAR

THERE IS/THERE ARE
There is one star for each state.
There are fifty stars on the American flag.

HAVE/HAS
How many stars does the American flag **have**?
It **has** fifty stars.

SINGULAR/PLURAL
There is one stripe.
There are thirteen stripe**s**.

BRANCHES OF GOVERNMENT

- **Simple Present Tense**
- **Have / Has**
- **Can**

VOCABULARY PREVIEW

the legislative branch   **the executive branch**   **the judicial branch**

1. the Capitol
2. the Congress

3. the White House
4. the President and the Vice President

5. the Supreme Court
6. the Supreme Court justices

Branches of Government

The government of the United States has three parts.
These parts are called the three branches of government.

The names of the three branches of government are
    the legislative branch,
    the executive branch,
    and the judicial branch.

Senators and representatives work in the legislative branch.
The President and the Vice President work in the executive branch.
The Supreme Court justices work in the judicial branch.

Check-Up

Vocabulary Check

branches	legislative	government	judicial	executive

1. The _____government_____ of the United States has three parts.

2. There are three _____ of government in the United States.

3. The President works in the _____ branch of the government.

4. Senators and representatives work in the _____ branch.

5. The Supreme Court justices work in the _____ branch.

Did You Understand?

Answer these questions based on the story. Use full sentences.

1. How many branches of government are there in the United States?

   _____

2. What are the names of the branches of government?

   _____

3. Who works in the executive branch?

   _____

4. Who works in the judicial branch?

   _____

5. Who works in the legislative branch?

   _____

Discussion

Describe the government in your native country: Does the government have different parts, or branches? What are they called? Who works there? Where is the government located?

The legislative branch of the government is called the Congress.
Senators and representatives are in the Congress.
They make the laws of the United States.
They work in the Capitol.*
The Capitol is a building in Washington, D.C.

The President and the Vice President work in the executive branch.
They enforce the laws of the United States.
The President lives and works in the White House.
The White House is in Washington, D.C.

The Supreme Court justices work in the judicial branch.
They explain the laws of the United States.
They work in the Supreme Court.
The Supreme Court is in Washington, D.C.

* The Capitol = the U.S. Capitol, the United States Capitol.

Check-Up

Matching I

1. senators and representatives

2. the President and the Vice President

3. the Supreme Court justices

the judicial branch

the legislative branch

the executive branch

Matching II

1. the executive branch

2. the judicial branch

3. the legislative branch

makes the laws

enforces the laws

explains the laws

Matching III

1. the Supreme Court

2. the White House

3. the Capitol

the executive branch

the legislative branch

the judicial branch

Answer These Questions

1. Who makes the laws of the United States?   _____

2. Who explains the laws of the United States?   _____

3. Who enforces the laws of the United States?   _____

Discussion

1. Describe how the government works in your native country: Who makes the laws?
Who are the leaders? Who works in the judicial branch? Is there a court like the
Supreme Court? What are the names and locations of the important government
buildings? (If you have pictures of these buildings, share them with the class.)

2. Discuss some U.S. laws you know about.

How Many Branches Does the United States Government Have?

A. How many branches does the United States government have?

B. The government has three branches.

A. Can you name the three branches?

B. Yes, I can. The legislative branch, the executive branch, and the judicial branch.

A. And which branch makes the laws of the United States?

B. Which branch makes the laws?

A. Yes.

B. Hmm. I think the legislative branch makes the laws.

A. That's right. And can you tell me who works in the legislative branch?

B. The senators and representatives.

A. That's correct. Very good.

A. How many branches does the United States government have?

B. The government has three branches.

A. Can you name the three branches?

B. Yes, I can. The legislative branch, the executive branch, and the judicial branch.

A. And which branch _____ the laws of the United States?

B. Which branch _____ the laws?

A. Yes.

B. Hmm. I think the _____ branch _____ the laws.

A. That's right. And can you tell me who works in the _____ branch?

B. _____.

A. That's correct. Very good.

Practice with another student, using the model dialog above as a guide.
Take turns asking and answering the questions.

1. enforces
   executive
   the President and the Vice President

2. explains
   judicial
   the Supreme Court justices

Check-Up

Grammar Check

Circle the correct answer.

1. The President   live   (lives)   in the White House.

2. Senators   work   works   in the Capitol.

3. The Vice President   work   works   in the executive branch.

4. The Supreme Court justices   explain   explains   the laws.

5. The President   enforce   enforces   the laws.

Questions and Answers

Practice the different ways to ask these questions. Then write the answers.

1. Which branch of the government makes the laws? ⎱
    Which branch of the government does the Congress work in? ⎰

    _____

2. Which branch of the government explains the laws? ⎱
    Which branch of the government does the Supreme Court work in? ⎰

    _____

3. Which branch of the government enforces the laws? ⎱
    Which branch of the government does the President work in? ⎰

    _____

Listening

Listen and circle the correct answer.

1. White House   Capitol   4. Congress   Supreme Court

2. White House   Capitol   5. senators   the President

3. Congress   Supreme Court   6. senators   the President

Ask and answer these questions. Practice with other students.

1. What state do you live in?

2. What city or town do you live in?

3. Name the capital of your state.

4. Name the capital of the United States.

5. Do you believe in the government of the United States?

6. How many states are there in the United States?

7. How many stripes does the American flag have?

8. What are the colors of the American flag?

9. Who makes the laws of the United States?

10. Where does the President live?

11. How many branches of government does the United States have?

12. Name the branches of government in the United States.

13. What does the Supreme Court do?

14. Which branch of government enforces the laws of the United States?

15. Which branch of government explains the laws of the United States?

CHAPTER TEST

Choose the best answer.

Example:

The government of the United States has three
- Ⓐ senators.
- Ⓑ presidents.
- ● branches.
- Ⓓ laws.

A. BRANCHES OF GOVERNMENT

1. The President of the United States works in
   - Ⓐ the White House.
   - Ⓑ the Capitol.
   - Ⓒ the Supreme Court.
   - Ⓓ the legislative branch.

2. The Supreme Court
   - Ⓐ makes the laws.
   - Ⓑ enforces the laws.
   - Ⓒ explains the laws.
   - Ⓓ lives in the White House.

3. United States representatives work in
   - Ⓐ the judicial branch.
   - Ⓑ the legislative branch.
   - Ⓒ the White House.
   - Ⓓ the executive branch.

4. The Congress of the United States
   - Ⓐ makes the laws.
   - Ⓑ enforces the laws.
   - Ⓒ explains the laws.
   - Ⓓ lives in the White House.

5. The three branches of the U.S. government are the legislative, the executive, and
   - Ⓐ the representatives.
   - Ⓑ the senators.
   - Ⓒ the White House.
   - Ⓓ the judicial.

6. United States senators work in
   - Ⓐ the Supreme Court.
   - Ⓑ the executive branch.
   - Ⓒ the judicial branch.
   - Ⓓ the legislative branch.

7. The Supreme Court justices work in
   - Ⓐ the Capitol.
   - Ⓑ the executive branch.
   - Ⓒ the judicial branch.
   - Ⓓ the legislative branch.

8. The executive branch
   - Ⓐ enforces the laws.
   - Ⓑ makes the laws.
   - Ⓒ writes the laws.
   - Ⓓ explains the laws.

9. The Congress works in
   - Ⓐ the Supreme Court.
   - Ⓑ the judicial branch.
   - Ⓒ the White House.
   - Ⓓ the Capitol.

10. The United States Capitol is in
    - Ⓐ New York.
    - Ⓑ Los Angeles.
    - Ⓒ Washington, D.C.
    - Ⓓ Miami.

11. There are three branches in
    - Ⓐ the Congress.
    - Ⓑ the U.S. government.
    - Ⓒ the Capitol.
    - Ⓓ the Supreme Court.

12. Who DOESN'T work in the legislative branch?
    - Ⓐ The Congress.
    - Ⓑ The President.
    - Ⓒ Senators.
    - Ⓓ Representatives.

B. GRAMMAR & VOCABULARY

13. The Vice President works in the _____ branch of the government.
    - (A) judicial
    - (B) legislative
    - (C) executive
    - (D) White House

14. The Supreme Court justices _____ the laws of the United States.
    - (A) explain
    - (B) enforce
    - (C) make
    - (D) write

15. _____ and representatives are in the Congress.
    - (A) Supreme Court justices
    - (B) The President
    - (C) Senators
    - (D) The executive branch

16. The _____ is the home of the judicial branch of the government.
    - (A) White House
    - (B) Supreme Court
    - (C) U.S. Capitol
    - (D) Congress

17. The U.S. government _____ three branches.
    - (A) work
    - (B) works
    - (C) have
    - (D) has

18. Senators _____ in the U.S. Capitol.
    - (A) work
    - (B) works
    - (C) have
    - (D) has

19. The President _____ the laws of the United States.
    - (A) enforce
    - (B) enforces
    - (C) make
    - (D) makes

20. The President and the Vice President _____ in the executive branch.
    - (A) make
    - (B) makes
    - (C) work
    - (D) works

C. DICTATION

Listen and write.

1. _____

2. _____

3. _____

4. _____

5. _____

Civics Enrichment

Field Trip Preparation: Prepare for a visit to the local office of your representative in the U.S. Congress. Practice conversations with other students so you are ready for the meeting: introduce yourselves, tell where you are from, tell about when and why you came to the United States, describe what you are learning in school, and tell about your plans for the future.

Discuss with other students: What problems or issues are important to you? What do you want to talk about when you visit your representative? What opinions do you want to share?

Visit your representative online! Go to www.house.gov/house/MemberWWW.html —a list of all members of the U.S. House of Representatives with links to their websites. Visit your representative's website. What kind of information does it have?

CHAPTER SUMMARY

KEY VOCABULARY

BRANCHES OF GOVERNMENT

executive
judicial
legislative

PEOPLE

Congress
President
representative
senator
Supreme Court
   justice
Vice President

BUILDINGS & PLACES

Capitol
Supreme Court
Washington, D.C.
White House

QUESTION WORDS

how many
what
where
which
who

OTHER WORDS

called
can
enforce the laws
explain the laws
have – has
laws
live
make the laws
work

FUNCTIONAL EXPRESSIONS

Can you tell me . . . ?
Hmm.
I think . . .
Name . . .
That's correct.
That's right.
Very good.

GRAMMAR

SIMPLE PRESENT TENSE

They **work** in the Capitol.
The President **works** in the White House.

HAVE/HAS

How many branches does the government **have**?
The government **has** three branches.

CAN

Can you name the three branches?
Yes, I **can**.

THE CONGRESS
THE PRESIDENT
THE SUPREME COURT

- Simple Present Tense vs. To Be
- There Are
- Time Expressions
- Question Formation

4

VOCABULARY PREVIEW

the legislative branch

1. the Senate
2. senator
3. the House of Representatives
4. representative

the executive branch

5. the President
6. the Vice President

the judicial branch

7. the Supreme Court
8. the Chief Justice of the Supreme Court

The Congress of the United States

The Congress of the United States is the legislative branch of the government.
The legislative branch makes the laws of the United States.
The Congress has two parts: the Senate and the House of Representatives.

Senators work in the Senate.
There are one hundred senators.
There are two senators from each state.
A senator's term is six years.

Representatives work in the House of Representatives.
A representative is also called a *congressperson* (or *congressman* or *congresswoman*).
There are 435 representatives.
There are different numbers of representatives from different states.
States with many people have more representatives.
States with fewer people have fewer representatives.
A representative's term is two years.

 **Check-Up**

Vocabulary Check

| representatives | senators | congresswomen | two | legislative | six |

1. The Congress is the _____ **legislative** _____ branch of the government.

2. There are one hundred _____ in the U.S. Senate.

3. There are 435 _____ in the Congress.

4. A senator's term is _____ years.

5. A representative's term is _____ years.

6. Congressmen and _____ work in the House of Representatives.

Did You Understand?

Answer these questions. Use short answers.

1. Who makes the laws of the United States?

   _____

2. What are the two parts of the Congress called?

   _____

   _____

3. How many senators are there in the United States Senate?

   _____

4. How many representatives are there in the House of Representatives?

   _____

5. How many representatives are there from your state in the U.S. House of Representatives?

   _____

6. How long is a representative's term?

   _____

7. How many senators are there from your state in the U.S. Senate?

   _____

8. How long is a senator's term?

   _____

Who Makes the Laws of the United States?

A. Now I want to ask you some questions about government.

B. All right.

A. Who makes the laws of the United States?

B. The Congress.

A. And what are the two parts of the Congress called?

B. The Senate and the House of Representatives.

A. Can you name the two United States senators from your state?

B. Yes. They're _____ and _____.

A. And do you know the name of your congressperson in the House of Representatives?

B. Yes. It's _____.

Practice with another student. Take turns asking and answering the questions.

The President of the United States

The President of the United States is the head of the executive branch of the
  government.
The executive branch enforces the laws of the United States.
The President is the chief executive.
The President is Commander-in-Chief of the armed forces.

The President lives and works in the White House.
The President's term is four years.
The American people elect a president every four years.
The President can serve two terms.

The Vice President works with the President.
The American people elect the President and the Vice President at the same
  time.
If the President dies, the Vice President becomes the new President.

The name of the President of the United States is _____.
The name of the Vice President is _____.

Check-Up

Vocabulary Check

| White House | serve | armed forces | executive | elect |

1. The President lives in the _____White House_____ .

2. The American people _____ a president every four years.

3. The President is Commander-in-Chief of the _____ .

4. The President can _____ two terms.

5. The President is the head of the _____ branch of the government.

The Answer Is "The President!"

Practice these questions and write the answers.

1. Who is the chief executive of the United States? _____

2. Who is the Commander-in-Chief of the armed forces? _____

3. Who lives in the White House? _____

4. Who is the head of the executive branch of the government? _____

What's the Number?

1. A U.S. senator's term is ___6___ years.

2. A representative's term is _____ years.

3. The President can serve _____ terms.

4. Americans elect a president every _____ years.

5. There are _____ United States senators.

6. There are _____ representatives in the Congress.

The Supreme Court

The Supreme Court and other federal courts are the judicial branch of the government.

The judicial branch explains the laws of the United States.

The Supreme Court is the highest court in the United States.

There are nine judges in the Supreme Court.

They are also called Supreme Court justices.

They serve for life.

The American people don't elect the Supreme Court justices.

The President appoints them, and the Senate approves them.

The head of the Supreme Court is the Chief Justice of the United States.

The name of the Chief Justice of the United States is _____.

Check-Up

Did You Understand?

1. What is the highest court in the United States?

   _____

2. Which branch of the government is it in?

   _____

3. How many judges are there in the Supreme Court?

   _____

4. Who appoints the Supreme Court justices?

   _____

5. Who is the head of the Supreme Court?

   _____

6. What is the name of the Chief Justice of the United States?

   _____

Grammar Check

Fill in the blanks.

Where	What	How long	How many	Who

1. _____How many_____ senators are there in the Senate?

2. _____ is a representative's term?

3. _____ makes the laws of the United States?

4. _____ is the name of the Vice President?

5. _____ does the Congress work?

Now answer the questions.

Questions and Answers

Practice the different ways to ask these questions.

> Who's the Chief Justice of the United States?
> Name the Chief Justice of the United States.
> What's the name of the Chief Justice of the United States?
> Can you name the Chief Justice of the United States?

Now answer these questions.

1. Who's the President of the United States? _____

2. Name the Vice President of the United States. _____

3. What's the name of your representative in Congress? _____

4. Can you name the two U.S. senators from your state? _____

5. Who's the Chief Justice of the United States? _____

Listening

*On Line **A**, write the name of the President of the United States.*
*On Line **B**, write the name of one senator from your state.*
*On Line **C**, write the name of the Chief Justice of the United States.*

A. _____ B. _____ C. _____

*Now listen and circle **A**, **B**, or **C**.*

1. A B C   4. A B C

2. A B C   5. A B C

3. A B C   6. A B C

Civic Participation

Write a Letter

Write a letter about a problem or issue. In your letter, tell who you are, describe the problem or issue, and give your opinion. Send the letter to the president, your representative, or a senator. Their addresses are:

President _____
The White House
Washington, DC 20500

Rep. _____
U.S. House of Representatives
Washington, DC 20515

Sen. _____
U.S. Senate
Washington, DC 20510

You're the Judge!

You and your classmates are the justices of the U.S. Supreme Court. Discuss an issue that the Supreme Court is currently considering. Make decisions about the issue and share your opinions with the other justices.

Meet with your Representative in Congress

Call your representative's local office. Visit the office, or invite your representative to visit your class. During the meeting, introduce yourself, tell where you are from, and describe when and why you came to the United States. Describe what you are learning in school, and tell about your plans for the future. Give your opinions about problems and issues that are important to you. Then ask the representative some questions about his or her job.

Branches of Government

	Legislative Branch		Executive Branch	Judicial Branch
	Senators	Representatives	President	Supreme Court Justices
Number	100	435	1	9
Term	6 years	2 years	4 years	life
Place of Work	Senate	House of Representatives	White House	Supreme Court
Job	Make the laws.		Enforce the laws.	Explain the laws.

Study the chart. Then practice with another student, asking and answering questions based on the information.

Who works in the _____ branch of the government?

How many _____s are there?

How long is a/the _____'s term?

Where do/does _____ work?

What does a/the _____ do?

Now ask and answer questions about the names of people in the government.

Who's _____?

Name _____.

What's the name of _____?

Can you name _____?

CHAPTER TEST

Choose the best answer.

Example:

A United States senator's term is

- (A) two years.
- (B) four years.
- ● six years.
- (D) eight years.

A. THE CONGRESS, THE PRESIDENT, & THE SUPREME COURT

1. There are 435 congressmen and congresswomen in
   - (A) the White House.
   - (B) the House of Representatives.
   - (C) the Senate.
   - (D) the Supreme Court.

2. The two parts of the U.S. Congress are the House of Representatives and
   - (A) the White House.
   - (B) the Capitol.
   - (C) the Supreme Court.
   - (D) the Senate.

3. A United States representative's term is
   - (A) two years.
   - (B) four years.
   - (C) six years.
   - (D) eight years.

4. The President of the United States is
   - (A) the head of the legislative branch.
   - (B) the Chief Justice.
   - (C) the Chief Executive.
   - (D) the head of the judicial branch.

5. The American people don't elect
   - (A) Supreme Court justices.
   - (B) senators.
   - (C) representatives.
   - (D) the President and the Vice President.

6. The Chief Justice is
   - (A) the head of the legislative branch.
   - (B) the head of the executive branch.
   - (C) the head of the Congress.
   - (D) the head of the Supreme Court.

7. Each state has two
   - (A) congressmen and congresswomen.
   - (B) senators.
   - (C) representatives.
   - (D) Supreme Court justices.

8. The American people elect a president
   - (A) every two years.
   - (B) every four years.
   - (C) every six years.
   - (D) if the President dies.

9. The Supreme Court justices serve
   - (A) for four years.
   - (B) for six years.
   - (C) for eight years.
   - (D) for life.

10. The executive branch
    - (A) enforces the laws.
    - (B) makes the laws.
    - (C) explains the laws.
    - (D) writes the laws.

11. The President appoints
    - (A) the representatives.
    - (B) the Supreme Court justices.
    - (C) the Vice President.
    - (D) the armed forces.

12. Which sentence ISN'T true?
    - (A) The President's term is four years.
    - (B) The President is Commander-in-Chief.
    - (C) The President can serve four terms.
    - (D) The President is the Chief Executive.

B. GRAMMAR: Question Words

13. _____ senators are there?

One hundred.
- Ⓐ How long
- Ⓑ How many
- Ⓒ Who
- Ⓓ Do you know

14. _____ is the Commander-in-Chief?

The President.
- Ⓐ Where
- Ⓑ Which
- Ⓒ How
- Ⓓ Who

15. _____ is a representative's term?

Two years.
- Ⓐ How
- Ⓑ How long
- Ⓒ How many
- Ⓓ When

16. _____ does the Congress work?

In the Capitol.
- Ⓐ Who
- Ⓑ When
- Ⓒ Where
- Ⓓ How

17. _____ branch of the government explains the laws?

The judicial branch.
- Ⓐ Which
- Ⓑ How
- Ⓒ When
- Ⓓ Who

18. _____ do we elect a president?

Every four years.
- Ⓐ Who
- Ⓑ What
- Ⓒ How many
- Ⓓ When

19. _____ are the three branches of government?

The legislative, executive, and judicial.
- Ⓐ What
- Ⓑ When
- Ⓒ Where
- Ⓓ Who

20. _____ do the Supreme Court justices get their jobs?

The President appoints them.
- Ⓐ What
- Ⓑ Who
- Ⓒ How
- Ⓓ Where

C. DICTATION

Listen and write.

1. _____

2. _____

3. _____

4. _____

5. _____

Civics Enrichment

 **Civic Participation:** Field Trip or Classroom Visitor: Visit the local office of your representative in the U.S. Congress, or invite your representative to visit your class. (See page 80 for suggestions about what to do during the meeting.)

 **Internet Activity:** Online Field Trip to the U.S. Capitol: Go to www.house.gov—the website of the U.S. House of Representatives. Click on "Visiting the Nation's Capital." Then click on "Virtual Tour of Capitol." Go on the tour. What do you see?

 **Internet Activity:** Visit the White House online! Go to www.whitehouse.gov—the website of the President. Click on "Your Government." Read about the President's Cabinet. Read about the branches of government. In the News and Features section, click on "Photo Essays." Look at the photographs and read the captions. What do you see?

CHAPTER SUMMARY

KEY VOCABULARY

PEOPLE

armed forces
chief executive
Chief Justice of the
   United States
Commander-in-Chief
congressman
congressperson
congresswoman
judge
people
President
representative
senator
Supreme Court
   justices
Vice President

BRANCHES OF GOVERNMENT

Congress
executive branch
House of Representatives
judicial branch
legislative branch
Senate
Supreme Court
White House

QUESTION WORDS

how
how long
how many
what
when
where
which
who

OTHER WORDS

appoint
approve
at the same time
become
court
die
different
elect
enforce the laws
explain the laws
federal courts
fewer
government
head
highest
if
life
live
make the laws

many
more
name
new
part
serve
state
term
United States
work
year

FUNCTIONAL EXPRESSIONS

All right.
Can you name . . . ?
Do you know the
   name . . .?
Name . . .

GRAMMAR

SIMPLE PRESENT TENSE VS. TO BE

The President **lives** in the White House.
The President **is** the chief executive.

Who **makes** the laws?
What **are** the two parts of the Congress called?

THERE ARE

There are one hundred senators.

TIME EXPRESSIONS

A senator's term is **six years**.
They serve **for life**.

 84

TYPES OF GOVERNMENT
STATE & LOCAL GOVERNMENT
PUBLIC OFFICIALS
THE CONSTITUTION
THE BILL OF RIGHTS

5

- REVIEW: To Be • Simple Present Tense •
  Have / Has • There Are • Can •
  WH-Questions • Yes/No Questions

VOCABULARY PREVIEW

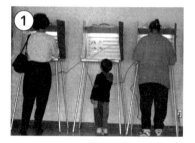

1. vote
2. voting machine

3. federal government
4. state government
5. local government

6. president
7. governor
8. mayor

The United States is not a dictatorship.
It doesn't have a dictator.
The United States is not a monarchy.
It doesn't have a king or a queen.

The United States is a republic.
It has a democratic form of government.
It has a representative form of government.

The American people vote for public officials.
They elect the President, the Vice President, the senators,
and the representatives.
These officials work in the United States government.
They serve the American people.

Check-Up

Vocabulary Check

elect	monarchy	democratic	republic	serve

1. The United States has a _____*democratic*_____ form of government.

2. The American people _____ representatives.

3. These representatives _____ in the government.

4. The United States isn't a dictatorship or a _____.

5. The United States is a _____.

Did You Understand?

1. What kind of government does the United States have?
2. Is the United States a monarchy, a dictatorship, or a republic?
3. Who elects the President and the Vice President of the United States?
4. What officials do the American people elect?

Grammar Check

Circle the correct answer.

1. The United States   isn't   doesn't   have a king or a queen.

2. The United States   isn't   doesn't   a monarchy.

3. The United States   does   has   a democratic form of government.

4. The American people   elect   elects   the President.

5. A representative   serve   serves   the American people.

How About You?

What form of government is there in your native country?
Do the people elect officials? Which officials?

State and Local Government

There are three levels of government in the United States:
   federal, state, and local.

The federal government has three branches.
Most state governments also have three branches.

The state legislature makes the laws of the state.
The state courts explain the laws of the state.
The governor is the head of the state's government.
The governor enforces the laws of the state.
The name of our state is _____.
The name of our governor is _____.

There are many kinds of local government.
There are cities, towns, and counties.
In some cities and towns, a mayor is the head of the local
   government.
Other cities and towns have a city manager.
The name of our city/town is _____.
The name of our mayor/city manager is _____.
The name of our county is _____.

 **Check-Up**

Vocabulary Check

| state courts | mayor | governor | state legislature | local |

1. The three levels of government in the United States are federal, state, and ___local___ .

2. The head of a state's government is the _____ .

3. The head of a city's government is the _____ or city manager.

4. The _____ makes the laws of the state.

5. The _____ explain the laws of the state.

Did You Understand?

1. What's the head of a state's government called?
2. Who makes the laws of your state?
3. What's the head of your city or town's government called?
4. What are the three levels of government in the United States?
5. What are the three branches of government in the United States?

Federal, State, or Local?

Discuss and decide which level of government is concerned with the following:

a. Driver's licenses
b. Garbage collection
c. Immigration
d. Public schools

e. Social Security taxes
f. Permission to build a house
g. Sales taxes
h. Parking regulations

A. What city or town do you live in?

B. I live in Anaheim.

A. Who makes the laws in Anaheim?

B. The City Council.

A. And what's the leader of the government in Anaheim called?

B. The mayor.

A. Do you know the mayor's name?

B. Yes. It's _____.*

A. What county do you live in?

B. Orange County.

A. And who makes the laws in Orange County?

B. The Board of Supervisors.

A. Can you name the governor of your state?

B. Yes. It's Governor _____.†

* Use a student's name here, unless you live in Anaheim.
† If you don't live in California, use a student's name.

A. What city or town do you live in?

B. I live in _____.

A. Who makes the laws in _____?

B. _____.

A. And what's the leader of the government in _____ called?

B. The _____.

A. Do you know the _____'s name?

B. Yes. It's _____.

A. What county do you live in?

B. _____.

A. And who makes the laws in _____?

B. _____.

A. Can you name the governor of your state?

B. Yes. It's Governor _____.

Practice with another student, using the model dialog above as a guide.
Take turns asking and answering the questions.

The Constitution

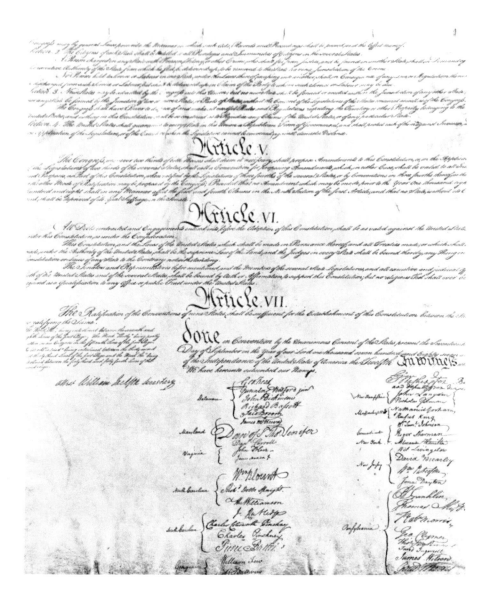

The Constitution is the highest law in the United States.
It is called "the supreme law of the land."

The Constitution gives the rules for the three branches of government.
It says what each branch can do and what each branch cannot do.
It tells the Senate and the House of Representatives how to make laws.
It tells the President and the Vice President how to enforce the laws.
It helps the Supreme Court and other courts explain the laws.
The Constitution also says that states can make their own laws.

The Bill of Rights

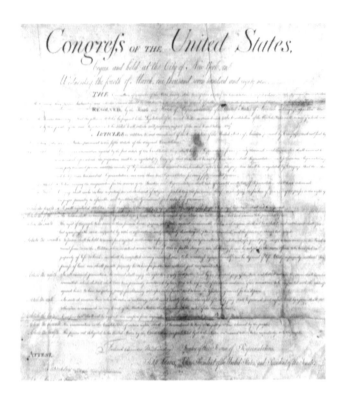

The people of the United States can change the Constitution.
Changes in the Constitution are called amendments.
There are 27 amendments to the Constitution.

The first ten amendments are called the Bill of Rights.
The Bill of Rights gives rights and freedoms to all people in the United States.

The 1st Amendment gives Americans many important rights.
It guarantees freedom of speech.
(Americans can say what they want to.)
It guarantees freedom of the press.
(Americans can write what they want to.)
It guarantees freedom of religion.
(Americans can worship as they want to.)
It guarantees freedom of assembly.
(Americans can meet together as they want to.)

 **Check-Up**

"Mirror" Questions

Practice these questions. Notice that they ask about the same thing.

What is the highest law in the United States? The Constitution.	What is the Constitution? The highest law in the United States.

Answer these "mirror" questions on a separate sheet of paper. Then practice asking and answering these questions with other students.

1. What are changes in the Constitution of the United States called?
2. What are amendments?
3. What are the first ten amendments to the Constitution called?
4. What is the Bill of Rights?
5. What is the supreme law of the land?
6. What is the Constitution of the United States?

Answer These Questions

1. Can the American people change the Constitution?
2. How many amendments are there to the Constitution?
3. Which amendment to the Constitution guarantees freedom of religion?

Bill of Rights Practice

These are very common interview questions about the Bill of Rights. Practice asking and answering them with another student.

1. Name one right guaranteed by the Bill of Rights.
2. Name two rights guaranteed by the 1st Amendment to the Constitution.
3. Name three rights included in the Bill of Rights.
4. Name four rights guaranteed by the Bill of Rights.
5. Name some rights included in the 1st Amendment to the Constitution.

Discussion and Debate

1. In your opinion, do all people in the United States have equal rights and freedoms guaranteed in the Bill of Rights?

2. In your opinion, should there ever be limits on freedom of speech or other rights? Why, or why not? Give examples.

B. GRAMMAR & VOCABULARY

13. There are 27 _____ to the Constitution.
    Ⓐ rights
    Ⓑ amendments
    Ⓒ freedoms
    Ⓓ laws

14. The American people _____ the President.
    Ⓐ serve
    Ⓑ vote
    Ⓒ elect
    Ⓓ work

15. The United States _____ a representative form of government.
    Ⓐ has
    Ⓑ does
    Ⓒ isn't
    Ⓓ doesn't have

16. The first ten _____ to the Constitution are called the Bill of Rights.
    Ⓐ representatives
    Ⓑ monarchies
    Ⓒ supreme laws
    Ⓓ amendments

17. The _____ is the head of a state's government.
    Ⓐ senator
    Ⓑ mayor
    Ⓒ governor
    Ⓓ representative

18. Americans can _____ as they want to because they have freedom of religion.
    Ⓐ talk
    Ⓑ worship
    Ⓒ meet
    Ⓓ write

19. The _____ makes the laws of a state.
    Ⓐ governor
    Ⓑ U.S. House of Representatives
    Ⓒ state legislature
    Ⓓ city manager

20. Freedom of _____ means Americans can say what they want to.
    Ⓐ speech
    Ⓑ assembly
    Ⓒ religion
    Ⓓ the press

C. DICTATION

Listen and write.

1. _____

2. _____

3. _____

4. _____

5. _____

Civics Enrichment

Field Trip: Visit your city hall or town government office. Meet with a local official. Take a tour of the building and learn about the services available in the different departments. Or visit your local government's website. What kind of information does it have?

"Class Election Day": Have an election in class. Run for class president or vice president. Give a campaign speech and tell students why they should vote for you. Or serve on the Board of Elections. Watch students vote. Count the ballots. Or be a TV news reporter! Interview the candidates and the voters, and report the election results.

Discuss: Why is it important to vote in elections? What are the "rights" of voters? What are the "responsibilities" of voters?

CHAPTER SUMMARY

KEY VOCABULARY

GOVERNMENT
branch
city
county
democratic
dictator
dictatorship
federal
form of government
government
king
level of government
local
monarchy
queen
representative
republic
state
state courts
state legislature
town
United States government

THE CONSTITUTION & BILL OF RIGHTS
amendment
Bill of Rights
Constitution
First Amendment
freedom of assembly
freedom of religion
freedom of speech
freedom of the press
freedoms
law
meet together
rights
rule
say
worship
write

PUBLIC OFFICIALS
Chief Justice of the
    United States
city manager
congressperson
governor
House of
    Representatives
mayor
official
President
public official
representative
Senate
senator
Supreme Court
Vice President

OTHER WORDS
build
change
driver's license
elect
enforce the laws
explain the laws
garbage collection
guaranteed
highest
house
immigration
included
makes the laws
parking regulations
people
permission
public schools
sales taxes
serve
Social Security taxes
vote
work

GRAMMAR

TO BE
The United States **is** a republic.
The United States **is not** a
    dictatorship.

SIMPLE PRESENT TENSE
The state legislature **makes** the
    laws.
The state courts **explain** the laws.

HAVE/HAS
The federal government **has** three
    branches.
Most state governments **have** three
    branches.

CAN
Americans **can** say what they want to.
Can you name the governor of your state?

THERE ARE
There are many kinds of local
    government.

WH-QUESTIONS
What city or town do you live in?

YES/NO QUESTIONS
Do you know the mayor's name?

DISCOVERY
COLONIZATION

- **Past Tense: Regular Verbs**
- **Past Tense: Irregular Verbs**
- **Did / Didn't**

VOCABULARY PREVIEW

1. Christopher Columbus
2. Native Americans
3. colonists
4. the *Mayflower*
5. Thanksgiving

Christopher Columbus

Christopher Columbus sailed from Spain in 1492.

He wanted to go to the Indies.

People in Europe liked things from the Indies.

Many Europeans traveled very far by land to get there.

Columbus hoped to find a better way to get there.

He wanted to sail there from Europe.

Columbus sailed west across the Atlantic Ocean.

He didn't land in the Indies.

He landed on some islands near the Atlantic Coast of North America.

In stories and in school, children often learn that Columbus "discovered"
   America.

But people already lived there.

Columbus called these native people Indians.

We now call them Native Americans.

Columbus shipped hundreds of the Indians back to Spain to sell as slaves.

Most of them died on the way to Spain or soon after they arrived.

He ordered the Indians to find gold.

He punished or killed Indians who didn't find enough gold each year.

Hundreds of thousands of Indians died in the years after 1492.

Check-Up

Vocabulary Check

| gold | Indians | Spain | Atlantic | islands | the Indies |

1. Christopher Columbus sailed from _____.

2. Columbus wanted to sail to _____.

3. Columbus sailed across the _____ Ocean.

4. Columbus landed on some _____.

5. Columbus called the people who lived there _____.

6. Columbus ordered them to find _____.

Grammar Check

Complete the sentences.

1. Columbus didn't sail to the Indies. He _____ to America.

2. Columbus didn't want to go to America. He _____ to go to the Indies.

3. The Indians didn't live in Europe. They _____ in America.

4. Columbus didn't land near the Pacific Coast. He _____ near the Atlantic Coast.

5. Columbus didn't order the Europeans to find gold. He _____ the Indians to find gold.

Pronunciation Practice

Say these pairs of words. Practice the past tense endings.

[t]	[d]	[ɪd]
hope – hope**d**	sail – sail**ed**	want – want**ed**
like – like**d**	live – live**d**	land – land**ed**
punish – punish**ed**	die – die**d**	

Pronunciation Check

Say these words and write them in the correct columns. Then say the words in each column again to practice the past tense endings.

shipped	discovered	liked	hoped	landed	called
died	wanted	traveled	sailed	lived	punished

[t]	**[d]**	**[ɪd]**
_____	_____ *discovered* _____	_____
_____	_____	_____
_____	_____	
_____	_____	
	_____	
	_____	

Maps, Journeys, and Discoveries

1. Using a map of the world, trace Columbus's route from Spain to the New World. Then, trace your own route from your native country to the United States.

2. Write a story about your journey to the United States. In class, share your stories with each other. Then, publish them for other students in the school, your families, and your friends.

3. Imagine you are a native person in the time of Columbus. Write a story about your life after Columbus lands on your island.

4. Tell about any explorers who came to your native country, and tell about the native people who lived there at that time.

The Jamestown and Plymouth Colonies

People from England first came to America in the 1600s.
These people were called colonists.
The original thirteen states were called colonies.

The first colony was in Jamestown, Virginia.
Colonists from England came to Jamestown in 1607.
They grew tobacco and traded with England.

In 1620 other colonists came to Plymouth, Massachusetts.
These colonists were called Pilgrims.
The Pilgrims came to America because they wanted religious freedom.
They sailed to America on a ship named the *Mayflower*.

Check-Up

Vocabulary Check

| tobacco | Pilgrims | colonies | freedom | England | colonists |

1. People from _____ came to America in the 1600s.

2. The original thirteen states were called _____.

3. The first _____ came to Jamestown, Virginia.

4. The colonists in Plymouth, Massachusetts, were called _____.

5. The colonists in Plymouth wanted religious _____.

6. The colonists in Jamestown grew _____.

Did You Understand?

Answer these questions.

1. What were the original thirteen states called?

   _____

2. Where was the first American colony?

   _____

3. Who came to Plymouth, Massachusetts, in 1620?

   _____

4. Why did the Pilgrims come to America?

   _____

5. What is the name of the ship that the Pilgrims sailed to America?

   _____

6. When did colonists from England first come to Jamestown, Virginia?

   _____

Grammar Check

Study these irregular verbs.

come – came	grow – grew

Now fill in the blanks with the correct words.

1. When did the first colonists from England _____ to Jamestown?

    They _____ to Jamestown in 1607.

2. What did the colonists _____ in Jamestown?

    They _____ tobacco.

3. Which colonists _____ to Plymouth, Massachusetts?

    The Pilgrims _____ to the Plymouth colony.

4. Why did the Pilgrims _____ to America?

    The Pilgrims _____ here because they wanted religious freedom.

Now practice the questions and answers with another student.

Listening

Listen and circle the correct answer.

1. a. In Jamestown, Virginia.
    b. In 1607.

2. a. In Jamestown, Virginia.
    b. In 1607.

3. a. Because they wanted religious freedom.
    b. In 1620.

4. a. Because they wanted religious freedom.
    b. In 1620.

5. a. The *Mayflower*.
    b. Plymouth.

6. a. The *Mayflower*.
    b. Plymouth.

Discussion

The Pilgrims came to America for religious freedom. Discuss all the reasons people come to the United States today.

How About You?

Answer these questions. They are common questions that people ask immigrants in the United States.

1. When did you come to the United States?

   _____

2. How did you travel to the United States?

   _____

3. Why did you come to the United States?

   _____

Information Exchange

Interview other students, using these questions. Write the students' names and information below.

> What's your name?
> (Could you spell that, please?)
> When did you come to the United States?
> How did you travel to the United States?
> Why did you come to the United States?

	Name	When . . . ?	How . . . ?	Why . . . ?
1.				
2.				
3.				
4.				
5.				

Another Perspective

Look at the bottom picture on page 103. Imagine that you are the Native American on the left. Describe what you are thinking and feeling as the Pilgrims land in the place where you live.

Thanksgiving

Life was very difficult for the Pilgrims in the Plymouth colony.
Many of them died during the first year.

The Native Americans helped the Pilgrims.
They taught the Pilgrims how to grow corn and other food.
They taught them how to fish.
They also helped them build houses.

The Pilgrims wanted to give thanks for the many good things they had in America.
They celebrated a holiday in the fall of 1621.
They invited the Native Americans to a big dinner.
The Native Americans brought most of the food.

This holiday in the Plymouth colony is called the first Thanksgiving in America.
(Actually, the Native Americans already had celebrations like this one.)
Today, Americans still celebrate Thanksgiving.
Thanksgiving Day is on the fourth Thursday in November every year.
Families come together and have a big dinner.
They usually eat turkey, potatoes, corn, squash, and cranberries.
The Pilgrims and the Native Americans ate these foods at their celebration in 1621.

Thanksgiving is a very special holiday in the United States.

✓ Check-Up

Vocabulary Check

invited	came	helped	celebrated	taught

1. The Native Americans _____ the Pilgrims in the Plymouth colony.

2. They _____ the Pilgrims how to grow food.

3. The Pilgrims _____ a holiday.

4. They _____ the Native Americans to a big dinner.

5. The Pilgrims _____ to Plymouth, Massachusetts, in 1620.

Did You Understand?

1. Who helped the Pilgrims in America?

   _____

2. How did they help the Pilgrims?

   _____

3. What holiday did the American colonists celebrate for the first time in 1621?

   _____

4. What did the Pilgrims and the Native Americans eat at their Thanksgiving celebration?

   _____

Pronunciation Check

Say these words and write them in the correct columns to practice the past tense endings.

sailed	invited	helped	celebrated	died	liked

[t]	[d]	[ɪd]
_____	*sailed*	_____
_____	_____	_____

108

Grammar Check

Fill in the blanks with the correct words.

come	came

1. The Pilgrims _____ together to celebrate Thanksgiving in the Plymouth colony.

2. Every year American families _____ together to celebrate the Thanksgiving holiday.

have	had

3. Americans usually _____ a big dinner on Thanksgiving Day.

4. The colonists _____ a big Thanksgiving dinner in 1621.

eat	ate

5. The Pilgrims and the Native Americans _____ turkey at their Thanksgiving dinner.

6. Americans usually _____ corn and cranberries with their Thanksgiving turkey.

How About You?

Write answers to these questions and discuss them with other students.

1. What holidays did your family celebrate in your native country?

   _____

2. How did you celebrate?

   _____

3. Do you celebrate Thanksgiving here in the United States? What do you do on that day?

   _____

Discussion

Life was very difficult for the Pilgrims in the Plymouth colony. Was life difficult for you when you came to the United States? What didn't you know how to do when you came here? How did you learn?

The Thirteen Colonies

The original thirteen states were called colonies.
These thirteen colonies were on the Atlantic Coast.

The first thirteen colonies were
New Hampshire,
Massachusetts,
Rhode Island,
Connecticut,
New York,
New Jersey,
Pennsylvania,
Delaware,
Maryland,
Virginia,
North Carolina,
South Carolina, and
Georgia.

Check-Up

Did You Understand?

1. What were the original states called?
2. How many original states were there?
3. Where were they?

Practicing the Colonies

Write out the names of the colonies in alphabetical order.

C <u>o</u> <u>n</u> <u>n</u> <u>e</u> <u>c</u> <u>t</u> <u>i</u> <u>c</u> <u>u</u> <u>t</u>

D _ _ _ _ _ _ _

G _ _ _ _ _ _

M _ _ _ _ _ _ _

M _ _ _ _ _ _ _ _ _ _ _

N _ _ H _ _ _ _ _ _ _ _

N _ _ J _ _ _ _ _

N _ _ Y _ _ _ _

N _ _ _ _ C _ _ _ _ _ _ _ _

P _ _ _ _ _ _ _ _ _ _ _ _ _

R _ _ _ _ I _ _ _ _ _

S _ _ _ _ C _ _ _ _ _ _ _

V _ _ _ _ _ _ _

Questions and Answers

Practice the different ways to ask these questions.

> Name one of the original colonies.
> Please name one of the original colonies.
> Can you name one of the original colonies?
> Can you tell me the name of one of the original colonies?

Now answer these questions.

1. Can you name one of the original colonies?
2. Please name two of the original colonies.
3. Can you tell me the names of three of the original colonies?
4. Name four of the original colonies.

Social Studies Enrichment

1. Compare the map of the colonies on page 110 with a map of the United States today. Are these states the same size as they were when they were colonies? Why not?
2. Prepare an oral report for the class about one of the states that made up the original thirteen colonies. Tell about the state today: its population, special geographical features, important cities, products, and places to visit.

Can You Name the Original Thirteen Colonies?

A. Now I want to ask you some questions about American history.

B. All right.

A. What were the original thirteen states called?

B. Let me see. . . They were called _____.

A. And what holiday did the American colonists celebrate for the first time?

B. _____.

A. That's right. And can you name the original thirteen colonies?

B. Hmm. I'm afraid I can't name all of them, but I can name a few.*

A. Go ahead.

B. _____, _____, _____,

_____ . . . Those are the ones I remember.

A. That's fine.

* If you can't answer a question completely, answer as well as you can.

Practice with another student. Take turns asking and answering the questions.

America (My Country 'Tis of Thee)

My country 'tis of thee,
Sweet land of liberty,
Of thee I sing;
Land where my fathers died,
Land of the Pilgrim's pride;
From every mountainside,
Let freedom ring.

—*Samuel Francis Smith*

The Macy's Thanksgiving Day parade is a popular holiday tradition.

Plimoth Plantation in Massachusetts is a living history museum. It has a Pilgrim village and a Native American homesite. Nearby there is a re-creation of the Mayflower.

Jamestown Settlement in Virginia has a colonial fort, a Native American village, and re-creations of the three ships that brought settlers to the Jamestown colony in 1607.

CHAPTER TEST

Choose the best answer.

Example:

The first American colony was in
- Ⓐ New York.
- Ⓑ Massachusetts.
- ● Virginia.
- Ⓓ Connecticut.

A. DISCOVERY & COLONIZATION

1. Christopher Columbus sailed to America in
   - Ⓐ 1942.
   - Ⓑ 1607.
   - Ⓒ 1776.
   - Ⓓ 1492.

2. Colonists from England first came to America in the
   - Ⓐ 1500s.
   - Ⓑ 1600s.
   - Ⓒ 1700s.
   - Ⓓ 1800s.

3. The Pilgrims sailed to America on a ship named
   - Ⓐ the *Jamestown*.
   - Ⓑ the *Mayflower*.
   - Ⓒ the *Plymouth*.
   - Ⓓ the *Thanksgiving*.

4. The Pilgrims came to America to
   - Ⓐ grow tobacco.
   - Ⓑ find a better way to get to the Indies.
   - Ⓒ have religious freedom.
   - Ⓓ trade with England.

5. Thanksgiving Day is always on
   - Ⓐ Thursday.
   - Ⓑ Tuesday.
   - Ⓒ Friday.
   - Ⓓ Sunday.

6. Columbus ordered the Indians to find
   - Ⓐ tobacco.
   - Ⓑ corn.
   - Ⓒ islands.
   - Ⓓ gold.

7. The Jamestown colonists
   - Ⓐ grew tobacco.
   - Ⓑ were called Pilgrims.
   - Ⓒ lived in Massachusetts.
   - Ⓓ sailed on the *Mayflower*.

8. Some of the original thirteen colonies were
   - Ⓐ Virginia, Massachusetts, and Florida.
   - Ⓑ Virginia, Massachusetts, and Texas.
   - Ⓒ New York, New Jersey, and Illinois.
   - Ⓓ New York, New Jersey, and Pennsylvania.

9. The Pilgrims' ship landed
   - Ⓐ in the Indies.
   - Ⓑ on an island near the Atlantic Coast.
   - Ⓒ in Virginia.
   - Ⓓ in Massachusetts.

10. Which state was one of the first thirteen colonies?
    - Ⓐ North Dakota.
    - Ⓑ West Virginia.
    - Ⓒ Maryland.
    - Ⓓ California.

11. Which state WASN'T one of the first thirteen colonies?
    - Ⓐ Maine.
    - Ⓑ Delaware.
    - Ⓒ Connecticut.
    - Ⓓ Rhode Island.

12. Which sentence ISN'T true?
    - Ⓐ The Pilgrims landed in Massachusetts.
    - Ⓑ The Pilgrims sailed on the *Mayflower*.
    - Ⓒ The Pilgrims grew tobacco.
    - Ⓓ The Pilgrims celebrated Thanksgiving.

B. GRAMMAR & VOCABULARY

13. The first thirteen states were called _____.
    - Ⓐ colonists
    - Ⓑ colonies
    - Ⓒ colonial villages
    - Ⓓ celebrations

14. Thanksgiving Day is a holiday in _____.
    - Ⓐ September
    - Ⓑ October
    - Ⓒ November
    - Ⓓ December

15. The Pilgrims and _____ celebrated Thanksgiving together in 1621.
    - Ⓐ Christopher Columbus
    - Ⓑ the Jamestown colonists
    - Ⓒ the Europeans
    - Ⓓ the Native Americans

16. Columbus traveled from _____ to America in 1492.
    - Ⓐ the Indies
    - Ⓑ Spain
    - Ⓒ the Atlantic Coast
    - Ⓓ England

17. Columbus _____ across the Atlantic Ocean.
    - Ⓐ lived
    - Ⓑ wanted
    - Ⓒ sailed
    - Ⓓ called

18. The Native Americans _____ the Pilgrims how to grow corn.
    - Ⓐ teach
    - Ⓑ taught
    - Ⓒ bring
    - Ⓓ brought

19. The Pilgrims _____ to America for religious freedom.
    - Ⓐ came
    - Ⓑ come
    - Ⓒ grew
    - Ⓓ grow

20. When _____ come to Jamestown?
    - Ⓐ do the colonists
    - Ⓑ does the colonist
    - Ⓒ did the colonists
    - Ⓓ are the colonists

C. DICTATION

Listen and write.

1. _____

2. _____

3. _____

4. _____

5. _____

Civics Enrichment

Field Trip: Visit a local supermarket. Talk with people there about the products they sell in the store. Look at the information on the shelves. Learn about unit prices and how to compare prices of products (or different sizes of the same product). Are there foods you like that the supermarket doesn't have? Tell the manager about these foods. Tell about any problems you and other students have when you use the supermarket.

Have a Thanksgiving celebration in your classroom! At home, cook some dishes with Thanksgiving foods such as turkey, potatoes, corn, squash, or cranberries. Use or adapt recipes from your native country, or use recipes for typical American Thanksgiving dishes. Bring the dishes to school, and have a holiday meal. During the meal, share your recipe instructions with the class.

Visit a colonial village online! Go to www.plimoth.org—the website of Plimoth Plantation in Massachusetts. Take the virtual tour. What do you see?

CHAPTER SUMMARY

KEY VOCABULARY

PEOPLE
children
Christopher Columbus
colonist
European
family
Indian
Native American
native people
people
Pilgrim
settler
slave

FOOD
corn
cranberries
potatoes
squash
turkey

PLACES
America
Atlantic Coast
Atlantic Ocean
colony
England
Europe
homesite
the Indies
island
Jamestown colony
Jamestown, Virginia
North America
Plimoth Plantation
Plymouth colony
Plymouth,
   Massachusetts
Spain
state
village

VERBS
arrive
bring
build
call
celebrate
come
come together
die
discover
eat
find
fish (v.)
get there
give thanks
go
grow
have

help
hope
invite
kill
land (v.)
learn
like
order
punish
sail
sell
ship (v.)
teach
trade
travel
want

OTHER WORDS
because
celebration
colonial
dinner
fort
gold
holiday
holiday tradition
life
Mayflower
parade
religious freedom
ship
Thanksgiving
Thanksgiving Day
tobacco

GRAMMAR

PAST TENSE: REGULAR VERBS

[t]	[d]	[Id]
hoped	sailed	wanted
liked	lived	landed
punished	died	invited

PAST TENSE: IRREGULAR VERBS

are – were
bring – brought
come – came
eat – ate

have – had
is – was
grow – grew
teach – taught

DID/DIDN'T

Why **did** the Pilgrims
   come to America?
He **didn't** land in the
   Indies.

THE REVOLUTIONARY WAR
THE DECLARATION OF INDEPENDENCE

7

- **Past Tense: Regular Verbs**
- **Past Tense: Irregular Verbs**
- **Did / Didn't**

VOCABULARY PREVIEW

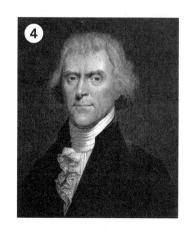

1. Boston Tea Party
2. George Washington
3. Declaration of Independence
4. Thomas Jefferson
5. parade
6. fireworks

Before the Revolution

England wanted to control its colonies in America.
The colonists in America didn't like this.

The colonists paid very high taxes to England.
The colonists didn't have any representatives in England.
They didn't like English laws, and they couldn't vote on those laws.

In 1773, England put a high tax on tea.
The colonists were very angry.
Some colonists in Boston, Massachusetts, went onto a ship that carried tea.
The colonists threw the tea into the water.
This is called the Boston Tea Party.

The colonists met in Philadelphia in 1774.
They decided not to buy English goods.
They wrote to the King of England and complained about English laws.
At the meeting Patrick Henry said, "Give me liberty or give me death."
The colonists prepared for war against England.

Check-Up

Vocabulary Check

| liberty | representatives | colonies | tea | taxes |

1. England wanted to control its _____ in America.

2. The colonists didn't have any _____ in England.

3. The colonists paid _____ to England.

4. Some colonists in Massachusetts threw _____ into the water in Boston Harbor.

5. Patrick Henry said, "Give me _____ or give me death."

Boston Tea Party Grammar Check

Study these irregular verbs.

> go – went
> put – put
> throw – threw

Now fill in the blanks with the correct words.

1. When did the English _____ a high tax on tea?

   They _____ a high tax on tea in 1773.

2. Where did some Massachusetts colonists _____ when England put a tax on tea?

   They _____ onto a ship in Boston Harbor.

3. What did those colonists _____ into the water?

   They _____ tea into the water.

Now practice the questions and answers with another student.

Discussion

The colonists didn't like the taxes they had to pay to England. What do you pay taxes on? What is this money used for?

The Revolutionary War

The Revolutionary War began in 1775.
It ended in 1783.
The American colonies fought against England.

The colonies fought the war because they didn't like English taxes, they didn't
    like English laws, and they didn't have any representatives in England.
The colonists didn't want England to control the colonies.
The colonists wanted to be independent.

The leader of the Colonial Army was George Washington.
The colonies won the war.

Check-Up

Grammar Check

Study these irregular verbs.

begin	–	began
fight	–	fought
win	–	won

Now fill in the blanks with the correct words.

1. When did the Revolutionary War _____?

    It _____ in 1775.

2. What country did the American colonies _____ against during the Revolutionary War?

    The colonies _____ against England.

3. Did the Americans _____ the war?

    Yes, they did. They _____ the war in 1783.

Now practice the questions and answers with another student.

Did You Understand?

Answer these questions.

1. What country did we fight during the Revolutionary War?

    _____

2. Why did the American colonies fight the war?

    _____

3. Who was the leader of the colonists' army?

    _____

4. Who said, "Give me liberty or give me death"?

    _____

The American colonists didn't want England to control the colonies.
The colonists wanted to be independent.
They wanted to be independent of England.

The Revolutionary War began in 1775.
In 1776 the colonists met at Independence Hall in Philadelphia.
They decided to declare their independence.
Thomas Jefferson wrote the Declaration of Independence.
The Declaration of Independence said that the colonies were free and
    independent of England.
Representatives of all thirteen colonies signed the Declaration of
    Independence on July 4, 1776.

 **Check-Up**

Grammar Check

Study these irregular verbs.

> meet – met
> say – said
> write – wrote

Now fill in the blanks with the correct words.

1. Where did the colonists _____ to declare their independence?

    They _____ at Independence Hall in Philadelphia.

2. When did Thomas Jefferson _____ the Declaration of Independence?

    Jefferson _____ the Declaration of Independence in 1776.

3. What did the Declaration of Independence _____?

    It _____ that the colonies were free and independent of England.

Questions and Answers

Practice the different ways to ask these questions. Then write the answers.

1.
    Who wrote the Declaration of Independence?
    Who was the writer of the Declaration of Independence?
    Who was the author of the Declaration of Independence?

    _____

2.
    When did the American colonies declare their independence?
    When did the American colonies sign the Declaration of Independence?
    When did the American colonies adopt the Declaration of Independence?
    When was the Declaration of Independence signed?
    When was the Declaration of Independence adopted?

    _____

IN CONGRESS. JULY 4, 1776.

The unanimous Declaration of the thirteen united States of America.

The Declaration of Independence is a very important document in
   American history.
It says that all people are created equal.
This is the basic belief of the Declaration of Independence.

It says that all people have rights that nobody can take away.
These rights are life, liberty, and the pursuit of happiness.

It says that the people tell their government what to do.
The government must do what the people say.
If the people want to, they can form a new government.

Based on these beliefs, the thirteen American colonies declared their
   independence.
They signed the Declaration of Independence on July 4, 1776.

Check-Up

Vocabulary Check

| government | document | independence | liberty | belief |

1. The Declaration of Independence is a very important _____.

2. The basic _____ of the Declaration of Independence is that all people are created equal.

3. The _____ must do what the people say.

4. The rights in the Declaration of Independence are life, _____, and the pursuit of happiness.

5. The colonies declared their _____ on July 4, 1776.

Listening

Listen and circle the correct answer.

1. a. At Independence Hall in Philadelphia.
   b. On July 4, 1776.
   c. To be free and independent of England.

2. a. At Independence Hall in Philadelphia.
   b. On July 4, 1776.
   c. To be free and independent of England.

3. a. At Independence Hall in Philadelphia.
   b. On July 4, 1776.
   c. To be free and independent of England.

4. a. England.
   b. From 1775 to 1783.
   c. They wanted to be independent of England.

5. a. England.
   b. From 1775 to 1783.
   c. They wanted to be independent of England.

6. a. England.
   b. From 1775 to 1783.
   c. They wanted to be independent of England.

How About You?

Discuss these questions with other students.

Is your native country independent?
Was there a revolutionary war in your native country? When?
Who did the people fight against?
Were there any famous revolutionary heroes?

Thomas Jefferson wrote the Declaration of Independence.

The thirteen colonies signed the Declaration of Independence at
   Independence Hall in Philadelphia on July 4, 1776.

Jefferson's words are very beautiful.

This is the most famous part of the Declaration of Independence.

> We hold these truths to be self-evident,
> that all men are created equal,
> that they are endowed by their Creator
> with certain unalienable rights,
> that among these are life, liberty, and
> the pursuit of happiness.

* For enrichment and speaking practice. Not required for the citizenship exam.

Did You Say *When* or *Where*?

A. Where did the colonists sign the Declaration of Independence?

B. Excuse me. Did you say *when* or *where*?

A. Where?

B. At _____ in _____.

A. When was the Declaration of Independence adopted?

B. Excuse me. Did you say *when* or *where*?

A. When?

B. On _____.

Practice these two dialogs with another student. Take turns asking and answering the questions.

Independence Day (The Fourth of July)

Every year on July 4th, Americans celebrate a national holiday.
The holiday is called Independence Day.
It is also called the Fourth of July.
On this day, Americans celebrate the birthday of the United States.
It's the country's birthday because on July 4, 1776, the thirteen colonies
   declared their independence.

Independence Day is a very happy celebration.
Many Americans get together with family and friends.
It is a summer holiday, and many Americans have picnics and barbecues
   outside.
In many cities and towns, there are parades and band concerts, and in the
   evening there are fireworks.

How do *you* celebrate Independence Day here in the United States?
Is there a celebration like Independence Day in your native country? When?
How do people celebrate the holiday?

Could You Please Say That Again?

A. Who was the main writer of the Declaration of Independence?

B. I'm sorry. I didn't understand. Could you please say that again?

A. Who wrote the Declaration of Independence?

B. _____.

A. What is the basic belief of the Declaration of Independence?

B. I'm sorry. I didn't understand. Could you please say that again?

A. What does the Declaration of Independence say?

B. It says that _____.

Practice with another student. Take turns asking and answering the questions.

A. Now I want to ask you some questions about the American Revolution.

B. All right.

A. Do you know what country we fought during the Revolutionary War?

B. Yes. It was _____.

A. And can you tell me who the leader of the Colonial Army was?

B. Yes. It was _____.

A. How many people signed the Declaration of Independence?

B. Hmm. I'm afraid I don't know. But I know that _____ wrote it.*

A. That's right. Can you tell me anything else about the Declaration of Independence?

B. Yes. _____.

A. Very good.

* If you can't answer a question, try to give other information to show that you studied this subject. (You do not need to know how many people signed the Declaration!)

Practice with another student. Take turns asking and answering the questions.

Review

Talking Time Line: Important Dates in U.S. History

Write these events on the correct lines in the time line below.

> Colonists came to Jamestown, Virginia.
> The Revolutionary War began.
> Columbus sailed to America.
> The colonies declared their independence.
> Pilgrims came to the Plymouth Colony.
> The Revolutionary War ended.

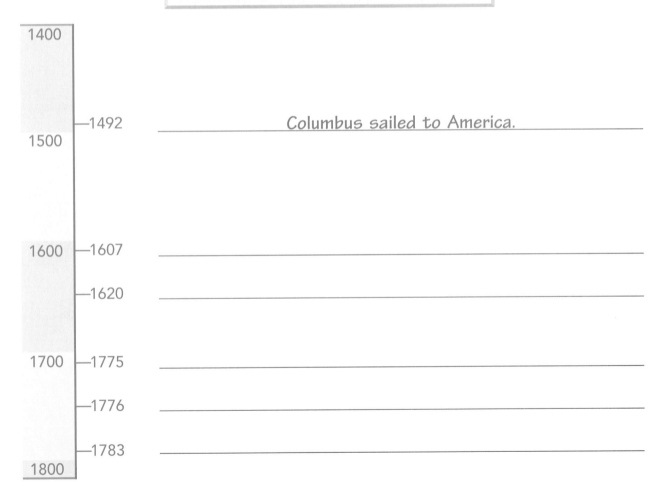

1400		
	—1492	Columbus sailed to America.
1500		
1600	—1607	
	—1620	
1700	—1775	
	—1776	
	—1783	
1800		

Now practice with another student, asking and answering questions based on the time line.

> When did _____ ?
>
> What happened in _____ ?

CHAPTER TEST

Choose the best answer.

Example:

In the Revolutionary War, the American colonies fought against

- Ⓐ France.
- ● England.
- © New York.
- Ⓓ Philadelphia.

A. COMPLETE THE SENTENCES

1. The Revolutionary War began in
   - Ⓐ 1607.
   - Ⓑ 1620.
   - © 1775.
   - Ⓓ 1783.

2. The colonies declared their independence in
   - Ⓐ 1620.
   - Ⓑ 1775.
   - © 1776.
   - Ⓓ 1783.

3. George Washington was the leader of
   - Ⓐ the Colonial Army.
   - Ⓑ the English Army.
   - © the Plymouth Colony.
   - Ⓓ the Jamestown Colony.

4. In 1776 the colonists met at Independence Hall in
   - Ⓐ Washington, D.C.
   - Ⓑ Boston.
   - © Chicago.
   - Ⓓ Philadelphia.

5. The national holiday on July 4 is
   - Ⓐ the Boston Tea Party.
   - Ⓑ Thanksgiving.
   - © Columbus Day.
   - Ⓓ Independence Day.

6. The rights in the Declaration of Independence are life, liberty, and the pursuit of
   - Ⓐ English tea.
   - Ⓑ documents.
   - © happiness.
   - Ⓓ war.

7. The American colonists wanted to be independent of
   - Ⓐ England.
   - Ⓑ France.
   - © the Colonial Army.
   - Ⓓ the United States.

8. The colonists fought because they didn't like
   - Ⓐ independence.
   - Ⓑ English laws.
   - © tea.
   - Ⓓ the Colonial Army.

9. The Fourth of July is
   - Ⓐ George Washington's birthday.
   - Ⓑ Thomas Jefferson's birthday.
   - © the birthday of the United States.
   - Ⓓ Patrick Henry's birthday.

10. In 1773 colonists threw tea into the water in
    - Ⓐ New York.
    - Ⓑ Boston.
    - © Philadelphia.
    - Ⓓ Baltimore.

11. On July 4, 1776, the colonists
    - Ⓐ had fireworks.
    - Ⓑ had picnics and parades.
    - © declared their independence.
    - Ⓓ had tea parties.

12. On July 4, 1776, representatives of all thirteen colonies signed
    - Ⓐ the Constitution.
    - Ⓑ the Declaration of Independence.
    - © the Pledge of Allegiance.
    - Ⓓ the Star-Spangled Banner.

B. ANSWER THE QUESTIONS

13. Who said, "Give me liberty or give me death"?
    - (A) Patrick Henry.
    - (B) George Washington.
    - (C) Thomas Jefferson.
    - (D) Abraham Lincoln.

14. When do people in the United States celebrate Independence Day?
    - (A) January 1.
    - (B) June 4.
    - (C) July 1.
    - (D) July 4.

15. Where did the colonies sign the Declaration of Independence?
    - (A) Boston.
    - (B) Philadelphia.
    - (C) Baltimore.
    - (D) New York.

16. Which sentence ɪsɴ'ᴛ true?
    - (A) The colonists paid taxes to England.
    - (B) The colonists had representatives in the English government.
    - (C) The colonists wanted to be independent.
    - (D) The colonies won the war against England.

17. What is the basic belief of the Declaration of Independence?
    - (A) America is a beautiful country.
    - (B) The government must tell people what to do.
    - (C) All people are created equal.
    - (D) People in England don't have rights.

18. Who wrote the Declaration of Independence?
    - (A) Thomas Jefferson.
    - (B) George Washington.
    - (C) Patrick Henry.
    - (D) Abraham Lincoln.

19. When did the Revolutionary War end?
    - (A) 1620.
    - (B) 1775.
    - (C) 1776.
    - (D) 1783.

20. Which belief ɪsɴ'ᴛ part of the Declaration of Independence?
    - (A) All people have rights that nobody can take away.
    - (B) All people are created equal.
    - (C) The people can form a new government.
    - (D) The people must have parades on July 4.

C. DICTATION

Listen and write.

1. _____

2. _____

3. _____

4. _____

5. _____

Civics Enrichment

What kinds of taxes do people pay to your local government? What does the local government do with this money? Get information from your city hall, town hall, or other government office. As a class, make a chart showing local government services and how much they cost.

Time Line Bulletin Board Project: As a class, make a large time line on a bulletin board. On the time line, show events that happened in the history of students' countries. Also show the events in U.S. history that you studied in this chapter. Draw pictures of the events and write paragraphs about them.

Visit historic Philadelphia online! Go to www.ushistory.org/tour/index.html— the website of the Independence Hall Association. Take the virtual tour, or click on these places in the Index: Betsy Ross House, First Bank of the United States, Independence Hall, Liberty Bell. What do you see? Why are these places important in U.S. history?

CHAPTER SUMMARY

KEY VOCABULARY

PEOPLE

colonist
family
friends
George
 Washington
King of England
leader
Patrick Henry
representative
Thomas Jefferson
writer

PLACES

America
Boston
Boston Harbor
colony
England
Independence Hall
Massachusetts
Philadelphia
United States

EVENTS

band concert
barbecue
Boston Tea Party
celebration
fireworks
Fourth of July
holiday
Independence Day
national holiday
parade
picnic
Revolutionary War

FUNCTIONAL EXPRESSIONS

All right.
Could you please say
 that again?
Did you say . . . ?
Excuse me.
Hmm.
I don't understand.
I'm afraid I don't know.
I'm sorry.

VERBS

begin
buy
carry
celebrate
complain
control
create
decide
declare
end
fight
form (v.)
get together
give
go

have
like
meet
pay
prepare
put
say
sign
take away
tell
throw
vote
want
win
write

OTHER WORDS

against
American
angry
basic
because
belief
birthday
city
Colonial Army
country
death
Declaration of
 Independence
document
English
equal
famous
free
goods
government

high
history
important
independence
independent
law
liberty
life
meeting
nobody
pursuit of
 happiness
rights
ship
tax
tea
town
war
water

GRAMMAR

PAST TENSE: REGULAR VERBS

Representatives sign**ed** the
 Declaration of Independence.
The colonists want**ed** to be
 independent.

PAST TENSE: IRREGULAR VERBS

begin – began
buy – bought
fight – fought
go – went

have – had
meet – met
put – put
say – said

throw – threw
win – won
write – wrote

DID/DIDN'T

Where **did** the colonists
 meet?
The colonists **didn't** like
 this.

THE CONSTITUTION
BRANCHES OF GOVERNMENT
THE BILL OF RIGHTS
GEORGE WASHINGTON

- **Past Tense: Regular & Irregular Verbs**
- **Past Tense: Was / Were**
- **Present Tense Review**

VOCABULARY PREVIEW

1. the Constitution
2. the Bill of Rights
3. freedom of speech
4. freedom of the press
5. freedom of religion
6. freedom of assembly

The Constitution

The colonies in America won the Revolutionary War in 1783.
They were free and independent states.
But they had a problem.
The thirteen states had thirteen separate governments.
There wasn't one strong national government.

Representatives from the states met in Philadelphia in 1787.
They wrote the Constitution.

The Constitution established the form of government in the United States.
It established three branches of government: the legislative branch, the
    executive branch, and the judicial branch.
It described the powers of the national government and the powers of the
    state governments.

The Constitution is the highest law in the United States.
It is the supreme law of the land.

Check-Up

Vocabulary Check

| branches | supreme | Constitution | powers | colonies |

1. The _____ won the Revolutionary War in 1783.

2. The _____ is the highest law in the United States.

3. It established three _____ of government.

4. It described the _____ of the national and state governments.

5. It is the _____ law of the land.

Grammar Check

| was | wasn't | were | weren't |

1. After the Revolutionary War, the colonies _____ free and independent states.

2. They _____ colonies of England anymore.

3. There _____ a separate government in each state.

4. Before the Constitution, there _____ a strong national government.

5. Representatives from the states _____ in Philadelphia in 1787 to write the Constitution.

Questions and Answers

Practice the different ways to ask these questions. Then write the answers.

1. What is the supreme law of the land?⎫
   What is the highest law of the land?⎭   _____

2.   When was the Constitution written?⎫
   In what year was the Constitution written?⎭   _____

Discussion

Describe your native country's constitution. How is it similar to the United States Constitution? How is it different?

Three Branches of Government

The Constitution established three branches of government: the legislative branch, the executive branch, and the judicial branch.

The Constitution gave the rules for the three branches of government.

The legislative branch makes the laws of the United States.

The legislative branch is called the Congress of the United States.

The Congress has two parts: the Senate and the House of Representatives.

The Congress meets in the U.S. Capitol.

There are one hundred senators in the Senate.

There are two senators from each state.

A senator's term is six years.

There are 435 representatives in the House of Representatives.

The states have different numbers of representatives.

States with many people have more representatives.

States with fewer people have fewer representatives.

A representative's term is two years.

The Constitution gives many powers to the Congress.

One important power of Congress is the power to declare war.

The executive branch enforces the laws of the United States.
The President and the Vice President work in the executive branch.
The President is the chief executive of the United States.
The President is Commander-in-Chief of the armed forces.

The President signs bills into law.
The President appoints members of the Cabinet.
The Cabinet advises the President.

A person must meet certain requirements to become President.
The President must be a natural-born citizen of the United States.
The President must be age 35 or older.
The President must live in the United States for at least 14 years
    before becoming President.

The President's term is four years.
The President can serve two terms.
Americans vote for the President in November.
The President is inaugurated in January.

If the President dies, the Vice President becomes the President.
If the President and the Vice President die, the Speaker of the House
    of Representatives becomes the President.

The judicial branch explains the laws of the United States.
The Supreme Court and other federal courts are the judicial branch of
    the government.
The Supreme Court is the highest court in the United States.
There are nine Supreme Court justices.
The President appoints them, and the Senate approves them.
They serve for life.

Check-Up

Did You Understand?

Answer these questions.

1. Which branch of the government makes the laws?

   _____

2. Which branch of the government explains the laws?

   _____

3. Which branch of the government enforces the laws?

   _____

4. How many senators are there in the United States Senate?

   _____

5. How many representatives are there in the House of Representatives?

   _____

6. How many representatives are there from your state in the U.S. House of Representatives?

   _____

7. Where does the Congress meet?

   _____

8. Who signs bills into law?

   _____

9. Who is the chief executive of the United States? _____

10. Name one requirement a person must meet to become President.

    _____

11. What special group advises the President? _____

12. Who becomes President of the United States if the President and the Vice President should die?

    _____

13. What is the highest court in the United States? _____

14. How many Supreme Court justices are there? _____

15. Who has the power to declare war? _____

16. How long is a senator's term? _____

17. How long is a representative's term? _____

(continued)

18. In what month do we vote for the President? _____

19. In what month is the President inaugurated? _____

20. Why are there 100 senators in the Senate? _____

Your Government Officials

Fill in the names of these government officials.

The President of the United States: _____

The Vice President of the United States: _____

A senator from your state (1): _____

A senator from your state (2): _____

Your representative in the House of Representatives: _____

The Chief Justice of the Supreme Court: _____

Questions and Answers

Practice the different ways to ask questions about the government officials above.

What's the name of _____?

Can you name _____?

Name _____.

Do you know the name of _____?

Can you tell me the name of _____?

Who's _____?

Now practice asking and answering questions about government officials with another student.

Discussion

Bring in recent newspaper photos of some government officials and discuss their recent activities.

The Constitution of the United States is a magnificent document.
The Constitution established our system of government more than 200 years ago.
We have the same system of government today.

The introduction to the Constitution is called the Preamble.
The Preamble begins with three very famous words: *We the People.*
These three words describe the power of the people in the government of the
    United States.
The people give power to the government.
The government serves the people.

> We the People of the United States,
> in order to form a more perfect Union,
> establish justice,
> insure domestic tranquility,
> provide for the common defense,
> promote the general welfare,
> and secure the blessing of liberty
> to ourselves and our posterity,
> do ordain and establish
> this Constitution for the United States of America.

* For enrichment and speaking practice. Not required for the citizenship exam.

The people of the United States can change the Constitution.
Changes in the Constitution are called amendments.
There are 27 amendments to the Constitution.

The first ten amendments to the Constitution are called the Bill of Rights.
These ten amendments were added to the Constitution in 1791.
The Bill of Rights gives rights and freedoms to all people in the United States.
The rights of citizens and non-citizens are guaranteed by the Constitution and
the Bill of Rights.

The 1st Amendment guarantees freedom of speech.
It guarantees freedom of the press.
It guarantees freedom of religion.
It guarantees freedom of assembly.

Other amendments in the Bill of Rights guarantee the rights of people who are
accused of crimes.
They have the right to go to court, have a lawyer, and have a fair and quick trial.
The Bill of Rights also protects people in their homes.
The police need a special document from the courts before they can go into a
person's home.

 **Check-Up**

Matching

Match these 1st Amendment rights and their meanings.

_____ 1. Freedom of the press

_____ 2. Freedom of assembly

_____ 3. Freedom of religion

_____ 4. Freedom of speech

a. Americans can say what they want to.

b. Americans can worship as they want to.

c. Americans can write what they want to.

d. Americans can meet together as they want to.

Did You Understand?

1. Can the American people change the
   Constitution? _____

2. What are changes in the Constitution called? _____

3. How many amendments are there to the
   Constitution? _____

4. What are the first ten amendments to the
   Constitution called? _____

5. Whose rights are guaranteed by the
   Constitution and the Bill of Rights? _____

6. Which amendment to the Constitution
   guarantees freedom of speech? _____

7. Name four rights guaranteed by the
   Bill of Rights. _____

   _____

   _____

   _____

Discussion

1. How is the Bill of Rights important in our everyday lives? What can we do because of
   the freedoms guaranteed by the Bill of Rights?
2. Discuss examples from current events of rights and freedoms that are not allowed in
   some countries.

Let's See What You Know About the Constitution

A. Now let's see what you know about the United States Constitution.

B. All right.

A. Do you know what the Constitution is?

B. Yes. It's _____.

A. And what is the introduction to the Constitution called?

B. The introduction to the Constitution? Hmm. I'm afraid I don't remember.
   I studied that in my class, but I don't remember the word.

A. That's okay. That WAS a difficult question. It's called the Preamble.

B. Oh, yes. The Preamble.

A. Do you know what the first ten amendments to the Constitution are called?

B. _____.

A. That's correct. Tell me about some of the rights guaranteed by the Bill of Rights.

B. Let me see. _____

   _____*

* Talk about at least three rights.

Practice with another student. Take turns asking and answering the questions.

George Washington

George Washington was the leader of the Colonial Army during the Revolutionary War.

He was an excellent leader.

The American people respected him very much.

In 1787 George Washington was the leader of the Constitutional Convention in Philadelphia.

At this meeting the representatives wrote the Constitution.

In 1789 George Washington became the first president of the United States.

He served two terms.

George Washington is one of the most important leaders in American history.

Americans call him "the father of our country."

Check-Up

The Answer Is "George Washington!"

Practice these questions and write the answers.

1. Who was the first president of the United States? _____

2. Which president was the leader of the Colonial Army during the Revolutionary War? _____

3. Which president was the first Commander-in-Chief of the U.S. military? _____

4. Which president is called "the father of our country"? _____

5. Which president was the leader of the Constitutional Convention in Philadelphia? _____

Listening

*On Line **A**, write the name of the first president of the United States.*
*On Line **B**, write the name of the president of the United States today.*

A. _____   B. _____

*Now listen carefully and circle **A** or **B**.*

1. A   B   5. A   B

2. A   B   6. A   B

3. A   B   7. A   B

4. A   B   8. A   B

Review

"Mirror" Questions

Practice these questions. Notice that they ask about the same thing.

Who was the first president of the United States? George Washington.	Who was George Washington? The first president of the United States.

Answer these "mirror" questions on a separate sheet of paper. Then practice asking and answering these questions with other students.

1. What is the supreme law of the land?
2. What is the Constitution of the United States?

3. Which branch of the government makes the laws of the United States?
4. What does the legislative branch of the U.S. government do?

5. Which branch of the government explains the laws of the United States?
6. What does the judicial branch of the U.S. government do?

7. Which branch of the government enforces the laws of the United States?
8. What does the executive branch of the government do?

9. What are the two parts of the U.S. Congress called?
10. What are the Senate and the House of Representatives?

11. What are changes in the Constitution of the United States called?
12. What are amendments?

13. What are the first ten amendments to the Constitution called?
14. What is the Bill of Rights?

Reviewing Government Officials

Ask and answer these questions. Practice with other students.

1. What's the name of the President of the United States?
2. Who's the Vice President of the United States?
3. Name one of the U.S. senators from your state.
4. Can you name the two U.S. senators from your state?
5. Who's your representative in Congress?
6. What's the name of the Chief Justice of the United States?

CHAPTER TEST

Choose the best answer.

Example:

The colonies won the Revolutionary War in
- (A) 1776.
- ● 1783.
- (C) 1607.
- (D) 1620.

A. COMPLETE THE SENTENCES

1. The Constitution of the United States was written in
   - (A) 1776.
   - (B) 1620.
   - (C) 1787.
   - (D) 1775.

2. The Constitution of the United States was written in
   - (A) Philadelphia.
   - (B) Washington, D.C.
   - (C) New York.
   - (D) Boston.

3. Changes in the Constitution are called
   - (A) rights.
   - (B) freedoms.
   - (C) bills.
   - (D) amendments.

4. George Washington
   - (A) wrote the Declaration of Independence.
   - (B) was the leader of the Constitutional Convention.
   - (C) served one term as President.
   - (D) wrote the Bill of Rights.

5. There are 435 congressmen and congresswomen in
   - (A) the Supreme Court.
   - (B) the Senate.
   - (C) the White House.
   - (D) the House of Representatives.

6. The introduction to the Constitution is called
   - (A) the Bill of Rights.
   - (B) the Preamble.
   - (C) the Declaration of Independence.
   - (D) the 1st Amendment.

7. The Bill of Rights describes
   - (A) the three branches of government.
   - (B) the powers of the national government.
   - (C) the powers of the state government.
   - (D) the freedoms all people in the United States have.

8. The executive branch
   - (A) enforces the laws of the United States.
   - (B) makes the laws of the United States.
   - (C) explains the laws of the United States.
   - (D) writes the laws of the United States.

9. The President can serve
   - (A) two years.
   - (B) one term.
   - (C) two terms.
   - (D) six years.

10. The legislative branch of the government
    - (A) enforces the laws.
    - (B) explains the laws.
    - (C) makes the laws.
    - (D) signs bills into law.

11. The President appoints
    - (A) members of the Senate.
    - (B) members of the Cabinet.
    - (C) members of the House of Representatives.
    - (D) members of the U.S. Congress.

12. The first ten amendments to the Constitution are called
    - (A) the Bill of Rights.
    - (B) the Preamble.
    - (C) the Declaration of Independence.
    - (D) the 1st Amendment.

B. ANSWER THE QUESTIONS

13. Who signs bills into law?
    - Ⓐ The President.
    - Ⓑ The Senate.
    - Ⓒ The House of Representatives.
    - Ⓓ The Supreme Court.

14. Which branch of the government explains the laws?
    - Ⓐ The legislative branch.
    - Ⓑ The judicial branch.
    - Ⓒ The executive branch.
    - Ⓓ The Congress.

15. Who becomes President if the President and the Vice President die?
    - Ⓐ The Chief Justice.
    - Ⓑ The Cabinet.
    - Ⓒ The Speaker of the House of Representatives.
    - Ⓓ The Supreme Court.

16. Which sentence ɪsɴ'ᴛ true?
    - Ⓐ The Constitution is the supreme law of the land.
    - Ⓑ There are 22 amendments to the Constitution.
    - Ⓒ The Constitution established the form of government in the United States.
    - Ⓓ The Constitution gives the Congress the power to declare war.

17. How many amendments to the Constitution are there?
    - Ⓐ Four.
    - Ⓑ Ten.
    - Ⓒ Twenty-two.
    - Ⓓ Twenty-seven.

18. Which president is called "the father of our country"?
    - Ⓐ Thomas Jefferson.
    - Ⓑ Abraham Lincoln.
    - Ⓒ George Washington.
    - Ⓓ John Adams.

19. In which branch of the government does the Cabinet work?
    - Ⓐ The executive branch.
    - Ⓑ The judicial branch.
    - Ⓒ The legislative branch.
    - Ⓓ The Congress.

20. Which sentence ɪsɴ'ᴛ true?
    - Ⓐ The President is Commander-in-Chief of the armed forces.
    - Ⓑ The President appoints members of the Cabinet.
    - Ⓒ The President must be age 35 or older.
    - Ⓓ The President makes the laws of the United States.

C. DICTATION

Listen and write.

1. _____

2. _____

3. _____

4. _____

5. _____

Civics Enrichment

As a class, discuss how people in your community exercise their rights guaranteed by the 1st Amendment. What are examples of freedom of speech, freedom of the press, freedom of religion, and freedom of assembly?

1st Amendment Bulletin Board Project: As a class, make a bulletin board display about rights guaranteed by the 1st Amendment—freedom of speech, freedom of the press, freedom of religion, and freedom of assembly. Cut out newspaper headlines and photographs that are examples of these rights and display them on the bulletin board.

Discuss with other students: Sometimes there are limits on the rights guaranteed by the 1st Amendment. (For example: a person can't shout "Fire!" in a movie theater; in some cities young people can't get together in large groups in public places.) What are some limits on the rights guaranteed by the 1st Amendment? What's your opinion about these limits?

CHAPTER SUMMARY

KEY VOCABULARY

PEOPLE
Cabinet
chief executive
citizen
Commander-in-Chief
George Washington
leader
member
natural-born citizen
non-citizen
person
police
President
representative
senator
Speaker of the House
  of Representatives
Supreme Court justice
Vice President

PLACES
America
colony
Philadelphia
U.S. Capitol
United States

BRANCHES OF GOVERNMENT
Congress
executive branch
federal courts
House of
  Representatives
judicial branch
legislative branch
Senate
Supreme Court

FUNCTIONAL EXPRESSIONS
All right.
I'm afraid I don't
  remember.
Let me see.
That's correct.

THE CONSTITUTION & BILL OF RIGHTS
Constitution
Constitutional
  Convention
document
First Amendment
freedom of assembly
freedom of religion
freedom of speech
freedom of the press
freedoms
introduction
Preamble
rights
supreme law of the
  land
system of
  government
We the People

VERBS
accuse
advise
appoint
approve
become
begin
change
declare war
describe
die
enforce the laws
establish
explain the laws
give
go to court
guarantee
have
inaugurate
live
make the laws
meet
respect
serve
sign
vote
win
work
write

OTHER WORDS
age
American history
armed forces
bill
Colonial Army
court
crime
excellent
form
free
government
important
independent
law
lawyer
life
magnificent
national
powers
requirement
Revolutionary War
rule
separate
special
state
strong
term
trial

GRAMMAR

PAST TENSE: IRREGULAR VERBS
become – became   meet – met
give – gave   win – won
have – had   write – wrote

PAST TENSE: WAS/WERE
There **was** a separate government in each state.
The colonies **were** free and independent states.

THE NATIONAL ANTHEM
EXPANSION
THE CIVIL WAR
ABRAHAM LINCOLN
AMENDMENTS

- **Past Tense**
- **Ordinal Numbers**

VOCABULARY PREVIEW

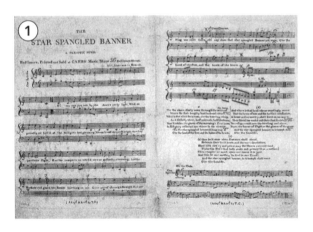

1. national anthem
2. the Civil War

3. Abraham Lincoln
4. Lincoln's Gettysburg Address

The National Anthem

The *Star-Spangled Banner* is the national anthem of the United States.
Francis Scott Key wrote the *Star-Spangled Banner*.
The song is about the flag of the United States.

The United States and England fought against each other in the War of
1812.
During the war, the British burned the White House and the Capitol
Building.
Then at night they attacked an American fort in Baltimore Harbor.
Francis Scott Key watched the battle.
He watched the American flag at the fort.
The next morning the flag was still there.
The Americans won the battle.
Key wrote about this in the *Star-Spangled Banner*.

The Star-Spangled Banner (The National Anthem)

Oh, say, can you see,
by the dawn's early light,
What so proudly we hailed
at the twilight's last gleaming?
Whose broad stripes and bright stars,
through the perilous fight,
O'er the ramparts we watched,
were so gallantly streaming?
And the rockets' red glare,
the bombs bursting in air,
Gave proof through the night
that our flag was still there.
Oh, say, does that star-spangled
banner yet wave
O'er the land of the free
and the home of the brave?

Firefighters display the American flag on the Pentagon in Arlington, Virginia, after the terrorist attack on September 11, 2001.

Practice reading and singing the Star-Spangled Banner *with other students.*

Your Native Country's National Anthem

Does your native country have a national anthem?
What's the name of the national anthem?
Who wrote it?
When do people sing it?
Sing your native country's national anthem in class.

Expansion

In the 1800s the United States expanded to the Pacific Ocean.

Americans wanted more land for homes and farms.

They wanted to use the Mississippi River to transport their farm products.

After the Revolutionary War, the western border of the United States was
  the Mississippi River.

Then the United States bought the Louisiana region from France.

It bought Florida from Spain.

Texas and California became part of the United States after wars with
  Mexico.

The United States received the Oregon country after it signed a treaty with
  England.

Russia sold Alaska to the United States.

Hawaii became a territory of the United States.

Alaska and Hawaii are the 49th and 50th states of the Union.

Check-Up

Did You Understand?

| California | Alaska | Louisiana | Oregon | Florida |

1. The United States bought the _____ region from France.

2. Spain sold _____ to the United States.

3. Texas and _____ became part of the United States after wars with Mexico.

4. Russia sold _____ to the United States.

5. England agreed to give the _____ country to the United States after the two countries signed a treaty.

Answer These Questions

1. Why did the United States expand in the 1800s?

   _____

2. Which states became part of the United States after wars with Mexico?

   _____

3. What are the 49th and 50th states of the Union?

   _____

Your State

1. What's the name of your state?   _____

2. Was your state one of the original thirteen colonies?   _____

3. When did your state become a state?   _____

4. Name the capital of your state.   _____

5. Name a famous person in the history of your state. Why was this person famous?   _____

The Civil War

The Civil War was a war between the states in the North and the states in the South.

The North and the South fought the Civil War from 1861 to 1865.

The Northern states were also called the Union.

The Southern states were also called the Confederacy.

One main cause of the Civil War was slavery.

Slaves were African people who were forced to come to the United States.

They didn't have any rights or freedoms.

Their owners bought and sold them like property.

The Southern states said they needed slaves to work on the farms.

The Northern states wanted to end the system of slavery.

Another cause of the Civil War was economics.

The North had many new factories.

The South had many big farms called plantations.

The North and the South disagreed about taxes.

These taxes helped Northern factories grow, but they made Southern farm products more expensive overseas.

Abraham Lincoln was against slavery.

After Lincoln became president in 1861, eleven Southern states left the Union and formed the Confederacy.

The Civil War began in 1861.

In 1865 the North won the war.

Abraham Lincoln

Abraham Lincoln was the sixteenth president of the United States.
He was president during the Civil War.
He was the leader of the Northern states during the war.
Lincoln wanted to save the Union.
He wanted the Northern and Southern states to stay together.

Lincoln was against slavery.
In 1863 he signed the Emancipation Proclamation.
This document freed the slaves.

In 1865 the North won the Civil War.
Five days after the war ended, President Lincoln was assassinated.

Abraham Lincoln was a great president.
Americans celebrate Presidents' Day in February each year.
On this national holiday, Americans honor George Washington and
Abraham Lincoln.

Check-Up

Vocabulary Check

| slavery | Union | plantations | rights | Confederacy |

1. The Southern states were also called the _____.

2. The Northern states wanted to end the system of _____.

3. There were many _____ in the South.

4. Slaves didn't have any _____.

5. The _____ won the Civil War.

The Answer Is "Abraham Lincoln!"

Practice these questions and write the answers.

1. Who was the president during the Civil War? _____

2. Who was the 16th president of the United States? _____

3. Who was the leader of the Northern states during the Civil War? _____

4. Who freed the slaves? _____

Did You Understand?

The examiner might ask you very general questions about a subject. These questions might be short, but their answers might be long or difficult. Answer the two general questions below.

1. What was the Civil War?

_____

_____

2. Give two causes of the Civil War.

_____

_____

Lincoln's Gettysburg Address*

Abraham Lincoln was an excellent speaker.
He gave his most famous speech in Gettysburg, Pennsylvania, in 1863.
He spoke at the dedication of the Gettysburg National Cemetery.
Four months before this speech, 51,000 Union and Confederate soldiers died
there in the Battle of Gettysburg.

Lincoln's speech is called the Gettysburg Address.
It is one of the most important voices of freedom in the history of the nation.
These are the two most famous parts of Lincoln's address.

"Four score and seven years ago
our fathers brought forth on this continent,
a new nation, conceived in liberty,
and dedicated to the proposition
that all men are created equal."

" . . . (W)e here highly resolve
that these dead shall not have died in vain—
that this nation, under God,
shall have a new birth of freedom—
and that government
of the people,
by the people,
for the people,
shall not perish from the earth."

* For enrichment and speaking practice. Not required for the citizenship exam.

A. What's the national anthem of the United States?

B. _____ .

A. That's right. Do you know who wrote it?

B. Hmm. Let me think for a minute. I think it was _____ .

A. That's correct. Can you tell me who the president was during the Civil War?

B. _____ .

A. And what did the Emancipation Proclamation do?

B. I'm sorry. Could you please repeat that?

A. Yes. Abraham Lincoln signed the Emancipation Proclamation during the Civil War. Do you know what it did?*

B. Hmm. Oh, yes. It _____ .

A. Very good.

* When you ask the examiner to repeat a question, the examiner might change the question or add some information. The examiner is doing this to help you understand the question.

Practice with another student. Take turns asking and answering the questions.

Amendments to the Constitution

Changes in the Constitution are called amendments.
There are 27 amendments to the Constitution.
The first ten amendments are the Bill of Rights.
Other amendments to the Constitution are very important.

Soon after the Civil War, there were three important amendments.
The 13th Amendment ended slavery.
The 14th Amendment made all Blacks citizens of the United States.
The 15th Amendment gave Blacks the right to vote.

In 1913, the 16th Amendment established income taxes.
In 1920, the 19th Amendment gave women the right to vote.
In 1971, the 26th Amendment gave citizens eighteen years old and
   older the right to vote.
Eighteen is now the minimum voting age in the United States.

Ordinal Numbers

1st first	**11th** eleventh	**21st** twenty-first
2nd second	**12th** twelfth	**22nd** twenty-second
3rd third	**13th** thirteenth	**30th** thirtieth
4th fourth	**14th** fourteenth	**40th** fortieth
5th fifth	**15th** fifteenth	**50th** fiftieth
6th sixth	**16th** sixteenth	**60th** sixtieth
7th seventh	**17th** seventeenth	**70th** seventieth
8th eighth	**18th** eighteenth	**80th** eightieth
9th ninth	**19th** nineteenth	**90th** ninetieth
10th tenth	**20th** twentieth	**100th** one hundredth

Write the correct ordinal number.

1. Abraham Lincoln was the _____ U.S. president.

2. George Washington was the _____ U.S. president.

3. Alaska was the _____ state to become part of the United States.

4. Hawaii was the _____ state to become part of the United States.

5. U.S. citizens can vote after their _____ birthday.

6. The _____ Amendment gave women the right to vote.

Matching

Match the numbers of the amendments and what they did.

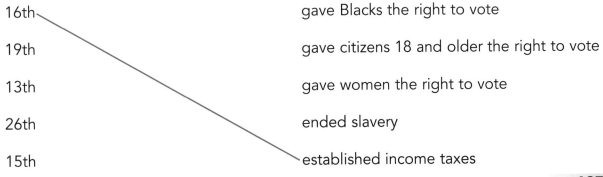

16th — gave Blacks the right to vote

19th — gave citizens 18 and older the right to vote

13th — gave women the right to vote

26th — ended slavery

15th — established income taxes

 **Check-Up**

Vocabulary Check

slavery	right	income	age	women

1. The 13th Amendment ended _____.

2. The 19th Amendment gave _____ the right to vote.

3. The 16th Amendment established _____ taxes.

4. The minimum voting _____ in the U.S. is eighteen.

5. The 15th Amendment gave Blacks the _____ to vote.

Questions and Answers

Examiners don't usually ask about a specific amendment (except the 1st Amendment). Usually they ask a general question, and you can choose which amendment you want to talk about. Practice the different ways to ask about amendments. Then write your answer.

> Tell me about two amendments that aren't in the Bill of Rights.
> Tell me about two amendments other than those in the Bill of Rights.
> Tell me about two amendments from the 11th Amendment to the 27th Amendment.

_____

_____

Listening

*On Line **D**, write the name of the president of the United States today.*

A. George Washington	**C.** Abraham Lincoln
B. Thomas Jefferson	**D.** _____

*Now listen carefully and circle **A**, **B**, **C**, or **D**.*

1. A   B   C   D   3. A   B   C   D   5. A   B   C   D

2. A   B   C   D   4. A   B   C   D   6. A   B   C   D

Talking Time Line: Important Dates in U.S. History

Write these events on the correct lines in the time line below.

The Bill of Rights was added to the Constitution.
The Civil War ended.
Representatives wrote the Constitution.
Women got the right to vote.
The Civil War began.
President Lincoln signed the Emancipation Proclamation.

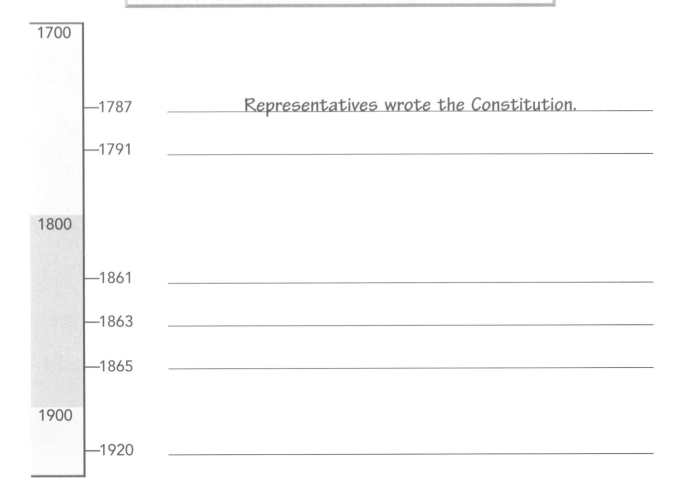

1700

—1787 _____ Representatives wrote the Constitution. _____

—1791 _____

1800

—1861 _____

—1863 _____

—1865 _____

1900

—1920 _____

Now practice with another student, asking and answering questions based on the time line.

When did _____ ?

What happened in _____ ?

CHAPTER TEST

Choose the best answer.

Example:

The writer of the *Star-Spangled Banner* was
- (A) John Philip Sousa.
- (B) Betsy Ross.
- (C) Bruce Springsteen.
- ● Francis Scott Key.

A. COMPLETE THE SENTENCES

1. The United States expanded to the west in the
   - (A) 1600s.
   - (B) 1700s.
   - (C) 1800s.
   - (D) 1900s.

2. The War of 1812 was a war between
   - (A) the North and the South.
   - (B) the United States and France.
   - (C) the United States and Mexico.
   - (D) the United States and England.

3. The United States bought the Louisiana region from
   - (A) France.
   - (B) Spain.
   - (C) Mexico.
   - (D) Russia.

4. The 16th president of the United States was
   - (A) George Washington.
   - (B) Thomas Jefferson.
   - (C) Abraham Lincoln.
   - (D) Ronald Reagan.

5. The Civil War was a war between
   - (A) the Americans and the English.
   - (B) the North and the South.
   - (C) the French and the Indians.
   - (D) the unions and the factories.

6. Texas and California became part of the United States after wars with
   - (A) England.
   - (B) Spain.
   - (C) Mexico.
   - (D) Canada.

7. The 19th Amendment gave the right to vote to
   - (A) women.
   - (B) Blacks.
   - (C) citizens 18 and over.
   - (D) immigrants.

8. The Civil War ended in
   - (A) 1783.
   - (B) 1812.
   - (C) 1861.
   - (D) 1865.

9. The 50th state of the United States is
   - (A) Oregon.
   - (B) Washington.
   - (C) Hawaii.
   - (D) Nevada.

10. The minimum voting age in the United States is
    - (A) 16.
    - (B) 18.
    - (C) 21.
    - (D) 26.

11. Abraham Lincoln was the president during
    - (A) the Revolutionary War.
    - (B) the War of 1812.
    - (C) the Civil War.
    - (D) World War I.

12. Abraham Lincoln gave his famous Gettysburg Address at a national cemetery in
    - (A) Massachusetts.
    - (B) Virginia.
    - (C) Washington, D.C.
    - (D) Pennsylvania.

B. ANSWER THE QUESTIONS

13. What is the national anthem of the United States?
    - Ⓐ The *Star-Spangled Banner*.
    - Ⓑ *My Country 'Tis of Thee*.
    - Ⓒ *America*.
    - Ⓓ *Born in the U.S.A.*

14. What document freed the slaves in 1863?
    - Ⓐ The Bill of Rights.
    - Ⓑ The Gettysburg Address.
    - Ⓒ The 15th Amendment.
    - Ⓓ The Emancipation Proclamation.

15. Which amendment gave citizens 18 and older the right to vote?
    - Ⓐ The 14th Amendment.
    - Ⓑ The 16th Amendment.
    - Ⓒ The 19th Amendment.
    - Ⓓ The 26th Amendment.

16. What did the 13th Amendment do?
    - Ⓐ It established income taxes.
    - Ⓑ It ended slavery.
    - Ⓒ It gave women the right to vote.
    - Ⓓ It guaranteed freedom of speech.

17. What region did the United States buy from Spain?
    - Ⓐ Florida.
    - Ⓑ Louisiana.
    - Ⓒ Texas.
    - Ⓓ Alaska.

18. What national holiday do Americans celebrate in February?
    - Ⓐ Independence Day.
    - Ⓑ Presidents' Day.
    - Ⓒ Thanksgiving.
    - Ⓓ Labor Day.

19. What were the last two states to become part of the United States?
    - Ⓐ Oregon and Washington.
    - Ⓑ Florida and Texas.
    - Ⓒ Alaska and Hawaii.
    - Ⓓ Alabama and Hawaii.

20. Which sentence ISN'T true?
    - Ⓐ One cause of the Civil War was slavery.
    - Ⓑ Eleven Northern states formed the Confederacy in 1861.
    - Ⓒ The Civil War ended in 1865.
    - Ⓓ Abraham Lincoln was the president during the Civil War.

C. DICTATION

Listen and write.

1. _____

2. _____

3. _____

4. _____

5. _____

Civics Enrichment

Work with a small group of students. Look at a copy of the U.S. Constitution. Find the amendments that you studied in this chapter. Then discuss ideas for a new amendment to the Constitution. As a group, propose one new amendment to the class. Give reasons why you think this new amendment is important.

Debate Activity: Have a classroom debate about the voting age in the United States. Divide into two teams. Each team should take one of these positions:
  a) The minimum voting age in the United States should be eighteen, as it is now.
  b) The minimum voting age should be twenty-one.

Visit online some of the historic places you learned about in this chapter! Take the virtual tours and look for other information about these places. Go to:
www.bcpl.net/~etowner/patriots.html—a website about the national anthem and the Fort McHenry National Monument in Baltimore, Maryland.
www.nps.gov/gett/home/htm—the website of the Gettysburg National Military Park in Pennsylvania.
www.nps.gov/linc/—the National Park Service website about the Lincoln Memorial in Washington, D.C. (You can click on the names of other memorials to learn about these places in the nation's capital.)

CHAPTER SUMMARY

KEY VOCABULARY

PEOPLE
Abraham Lincoln
African
American
Blacks
British
citizens
firefighter
Francis Scott Key
George Washington
leader
president
slave
speaker
women

EVENTS
battle
Civil War
dedication
Emancipation Proclamation
Gettysburg Address
national holiday
Presidents' Day
Revolutionary War
terrorist attack
war
War of 1812

PLACES, COUNTRIES, GEOGRAPHY
Alaska
Arlington, Virginia
Baltimore Harbor
border
California
Capitol Building
England
France
Gettysburg National
   Cemetery
Gettysburg, Pennsylvania
Hawaii
Louisiana
Mexico
Mississippi River
North
Northern states
Oregon
Pacific Ocean
Pentagon
region
Russia
South
Southern states
Spain
Texas
United States
western

VERBS
assassinate
attack
become
begin
burn
buy
celebrate
come
disagree
display
end
establish
expand
fight
force
free
give
grow
help
honor
leave
make
need
receive
save
sell
sign
speak
stay together

transport
use
vote
want
watch
win
work
write

OTHER WORDS
address
cause
Confederacy
document
economics
factory
famous
farm
farm products
flag
fort
freedoms
history
home
income taxes
land
minimum
nation
national anthem

overseas
plantation
property
rights
slavery
song
speech
Star-Spangled
   Banner
state
system
taxes
territory
treaty
Union
voting age

INDUSTRIAL REVOLUTION
LABOR MOVEMENT
IMMIGRATION
20th-CENTURY HISTORY
CIVIL RIGHTS MOVEMENT
CITIZENS' RIGHTS &
RESPONSIBILITIES
PRESIDENTS: 1961 – PRESENT
SEPTEMBER 11, 2001

- **Past Tense**
- **Can / Should / Must**

VOCABULARY PREVIEW

1. invention
2. labor movement
3. immigration
4. the Great Depression
5. the United Nations
6. civil rights movement

The Industrial Revolution

The first Americans were farmers.

In the 1790s the first factories opened in the United States.

The cotton gin and the sewing machine were very important inventions.

With these machines, the United States produced clothing much faster than before.

Americans also invented the telephone, the typewriter, the phonograph, and the light bulb.

The railroads went across the country, from the East Coast to the West Coast.

The factories were usually in cities, and the cities grew larger.

People came from the farms and immigrants came from other countries to work in the factories.

The Labor Movement

Factory workers had a difficult life.
They usually worked twelve hours a day.
Their pay was low.

Many workers got hurt because the factories weren't safe.
Workers began to come together in groups.
They formed labor unions.
These unions fought for better hours, better pay, and safer workplaces.
Many workers belong to unions today.

Americans celebrate Labor Day every year on the first Monday in
    September.
This national holiday celebrates the workers of the United States.

A Nation of Immigrants*

In the 1800s, America grew very quickly.
Expansion added new farmland, and the Industrial Revolution built new factories and cities.
America needed farmers and workers.
Immigrants came from many countries.
They worked on farms and in factories.
They helped build the cities of the United States.

In the 1900s, the United States began to limit immigration.
The government made many laws to stop immigration from many countries.
In 1965 a new immigration law changed this.
The law allowed immigrants to apply from any country.

Immigrants continue to come to the United States every day.
Some come here because life was difficult or dangerous in their native country.
Others come here because they want a better life for themselves and their families here in the United States.

Except for Native Americans, *all* Americans come from families of immigrants.
The United States is "a nation of immigrants."

*Information on this page is for enrichment and student interest. It is not usually required for the citizenship exam.

Check-Up

Vocabulary Check

| labor unions | clothing | sewing machine | laws | immigrants |

1. The _____ was a very important invention.

2. Workers formed _____ to fight for better hours and better pay.

3. America's farms and factories needed _____ from other countries in the 1800s.

4. In the 1900s, the country made _____ to limit immigration.

5. With new machines, American factories produced _____ much faster than before.

Did You Understand?

1. Name one important invention during the Industrial Revolution.
2. Why did workers form labor unions?
3. Why did the United States need immigrants in the 1800s?

Discussion

1. Where did people work in your native country in the place where you lived? On farms? In factories? In offices? What did you do in your native country before you came to the United States?

2. If you are working now, talk about your job. What are your hours? Is your pay good? Is your workplace safe? Is there a union? What can you do to make your workplace safer or better?

3. Why did you come to the United States? How did you get here? Did you come alone, or with your family? What did you do when you first came here?

4. Look at the photos on page 174. Describe the three different immigration scenes.

20th-Century History*

World War I

World War I began in 1914.

England, France, and Russia fought against Germany and Austria-Hungary.

The United States entered World War I in 1917 and helped England, France, and Russia win the war.

The war ended in 1918.

The United States became a great world power.

The Depression

From 1929 to 1939 there was a Great Depression.
The American economy collapsed.

The Depression had many causes.
Factories and farms produced too much.
After World War I, countries in Europe didn't have money to buy American goods.
Many people borrowed too much money.

It was a very difficult time in the United States.
Factories closed, workers lost their jobs or their salaries were cut, many banks closed, and many people lost all their money in the stock market.

* The many dates in this lesson are for your information. You do not usually need to know these dates for the citizenship exam, but you should know a little about each of these topics in 20th-century history.

Franklin Delano Roosevelt

Franklin D. Roosevelt was the president of the United States from 1932 to 1945.

He became the president during the Great Depression.

His plan to help the country was called The New Deal.

The government made jobs for people who had no work.

They built roads, parks, bridges, and buildings.

The government gave people loans to help them keep their farms or homes.

The Social Security system began.

Roosevelt was the president during World War II.

He served longer than any other president.

He died during his fourth term in office in 1945.

World War II

World War II began in 1939.

The United States, England, Russia, and other countries were called the Allied nations.

They fought against Germany, Italy, and Japan.

The United States entered World War II in 1941 when the Japanese bombed Pearl Harbor in Hawaii.

In 1945 the United States dropped two atomic bombs on Hiroshima and Nagasaki in Japan.

The United States and the Allied nations won the war in 1945.

The United Nations (The UN)

After World War II, many countries formed a new international organization called the United Nations.

It is also called the UN.*

At the United Nations, countries discuss world problems and try to keep peace.

The UN also helps many countries.

It gives them economic aid and provides education programs, health programs, and other assistance.

The Cold War, the Korean War, and the Vietnam War

After World War II, the United States and the Soviet Union became major world powers.

The two countries had very different political systems.

The American system is democratic, and the Soviet system was communist.

The United States and the Soviet Union did not fight against each other, but they competed with each other politically and economically.

This was called the Cold War.

The United States fought Communist forces in two wars.

From 1950 to 1953, the United States fought in the Korean War.

From 1964 to 1973, the United States fought in the Vietnam War.

The Cold War ended during the years 1990 and 1991 when the Soviet Union broke up into independent states.

* UN is pronounced "U - N."

 **Check-Up**

Vocabulary Check

| Depression | United Nations | Cold War | World War I | New Deal |

1. The international organization formed after World War II is called the

   _____.

2. _____ began in 1914.

3. Franklin D. Roosevelt's plan to help the country was called the _____.

4. From 1929 to 1939 there was a Great _____.

5. The United States and the Soviet Union competed during the _____.

Did You Understand?

1. What happened during the Great Depression? Why?
2. What was the New Deal?
3. When did the United States enter World War II? (After what event?)
4. What was the major difference between the American and Soviet political systems?
5. What is the UN?

Fact Check

Circle the correct answer.

1. The United States fought in the   Korean   Vietnam   War from 1964 to 1973.

2. Social Security   The Vietnam War   began when Franklin D. Roosevelt was the

   president.

3. The U.S. economy collapsed during the   Depression   Cold War .

4. The United States fought against Germany and   Russia   Japan   during World War II.

5. The Soviet Union had a   democratic   communist   political system.

Questions and Answers

Practice the different ways to ask these questions. Then write the answers.

1.   Name the president during the Depression.
          Can you name the president during the Depression?
                  Who was the president during the Depression?
     Can you tell me who the president was during the Depression?

     _____

2.   Which countries were our enemies during World War II?
     Which countries did we fight against during World War II?

     _____

3.   What countries were our allies during World War II?
        What countries did we help during World War II?
     What countries were on our side during World War II?

     _____

4. Name one purpose of the United Nations.
     Name one thing the United Nations does.
              What does the United Nations do?

     _____

Listening

Listen and circle the correct answer.

1.
   a. Abraham Lincoln.

   b. Franklin D. Roosevelt.

2.
   a. When the Japanese
       bombed Pearl Harbor.

   b. When the United States
       bombed Hiroshima.

3.
   a. Germany and Japan.

   b. The Soviet Union and
       the United States.

4.
   a. Germany and Japan.

   b. England and Russia.

5.
   a. The New Deal.

   b. The United Nations.

6.
   a. Factories and banks closed.

   b. World War I began.

The Civil Rights Movement

During the 1950s and 1960s, the civil rights movement worked to end
discrimination against Blacks in the United States.
It worked for equal rights for all Americans.

The Reverend Martin Luther King, Jr., was the most famous leader of
the civil rights movement.
He led protests against discrimination in many states.
In 1963 he led hundreds of thousands of people in a demonstration to
support new civil rights laws.
It was called the March on Washington.

In 1968 Martin Luther King, Jr., was shot and killed.
The civil rights movement and the nation lost a great leader.
The United States remembers Martin Luther King, Jr., in a national
holiday on the third Monday in January every year.

Martin Luther King, Jr.*

During the March on Washington in 1963, Martin Luther King, Jr., gave a
 very powerful and beautiful speech at the Lincoln Memorial.
It is called his "I Have a Dream" speech.
These are the most famous parts of what he said that day.

I . . . have a dream. It is a dream deeply rooted in the
American dream. I have a dream that one day this nation will
rise up and live out the true meaning of its creed: "We hold these
truths to be self-evident—that all men are created equal."

This will be the day when all of God's children will be able to
sing with new meaning "My Country 'tis of thee, sweet land of
liberty, of thee I sing. Land where my fathers died, land of the
pilgrim's pride, from every mountainside let freedom ring." And if
America is to be a great nation this must become true.

When we let freedom ring, when we let it ring from every
village and every hamlet, from every state and every city, we will
be able to speed up that day when all of God's children, black men
and white men, Jews and Gentiles, Protestants and Catholics, will
be able to join hands and sing in the words of the Old Negro
spiritual, "Free at last! Free at last! Thank God almighty, we are
free at last!"

* For enrichment and speaking practice. Not required for the citizenship exam.

Discussion

1. How do you think the civil rights movement of the 1950s and 1960s helps
   immigrants in the United States today?

2. In your opinion, is there still discrimination in the United States? Give reasons for
   your answer.

The most important right U.S. citizens have is the right to vote.

Citizens can vote for federal, state, and local officials.

Every four years, in November, citizens can vote for the president of the
United States.

They usually choose between a Democratic and a Republican candidate
for president.

The Democratic and Republican parties are the two major political
parties in the United States.

Citizens also have responsibilities.

They should vote,

     obey the laws,

     pay taxes,

     serve on a jury,

     and be active in their communities.

Citizens should know what is happening in their city, in their state, and
in the nation.

They should follow the news on TV, on the radio, or in the newspaper.

Presidential Profiles

John F. Kennedy

John F. Kennedy was the president from 1961 to 1963.

He was the youngest president in U.S. history.

He worked for civil rights.

He wanted to begin many programs to help poor people.

He sent soldiers to Vietnam.

President Kennedy was assassinated in 1963.

Lyndon B. Johnson

Lyndon B. Johnson was the president from 1963 to 1969.

He became president after Kennedy's assassination.

His Great Society programs helped poor people.

Important civil rights laws were passed during his administration.

The Vietnam War expanded.

Richard Nixon

Richard Nixon was the president from 1969 to 1974.
He began relations with China.
He ended the United States role in Vietnam.
He resigned because of a political scandal called
  Watergate.

Gerald Ford

Gerald Ford was the president from 1974 to 1977.
He was the first president not elected as president
  or vice president by the people.
He took office after President Nixon resigned.
The nation's economy was bad during his time in
  office.

James Earl (Jimmy) Carter

Jimmy Carter was the president from 1977 to 1981.
He worked for human rights for people in foreign
  countries.
He didn't have experience in national politics.
The nation's economy didn't get better during his
  time in office.

Ronald Reagan

Ronald Reagan was the president from 1981 to 1989.

He lowered taxes and spent more money on the military.

He worked to reduce the role of the federal government in regulating business, providing social services, and other aspects of U.S. life.

The nation's economy improved during his two terms.

Before he entered politics, Ronald Reagan was an actor.

As president, he was called "the great communicator."

George Bush

George Bush was the president from 1989 to 1993.

He served as vice president with President Reagan.

He continued many of the Reagan policies.

There was a recession during his time in office.

In 1991 he sent troops to the Gulf War, also called Operation Desert Storm.

He served one term as president.

William J. (Bill) Clinton

Bill Clinton was the president from 1993 to 2001.

He raised taxes, reduced government spending, and eliminated the national debt.

He increased federal money for schools and local police departments, and he reformed the welfare system.

He sent troops to Somalia, Bosnia, and Kosovo to support international peace-keeping missions.

He was involved in political and personal scandals.

In 1998 he was impeached by the House of Representatives.

In 1999 the Senate had an impeachment trial.

President Clinton was acquitted and stayed in office.

George W. Bush

George W. Bush is the son of former President Bush.

He became the president in 2001 after a very unusual election.

There was a problem counting votes in Florida, and the Supreme Court was involved in the solution more than one month after Election Day.

On September 11, 2001, eight months after President Bush took office, international terrorists attacked the World Trade Center in New York City and the Pentagon in Arlington, Virginia.

President Bush sent troops to Afghanistan to fight the terrorist organization responsible for the attacks on the United States.

September 11, 2001

On the morning of September 11, 2001, terrorists hijacked four airplanes
   from Boston, New Jersey, and the Washington, D.C. area.
They crashed two planes into the twin towers of the World Trade Center in
   New York City.
Both towers of the World Trade Center collapsed.
One plane crashed into the Pentagon — the headquarters of the U.S. armed
   forces, in Arlington, Virginia.
One plane crashed in Pennsylvania.
Thousands of people died in the buildings and on the airplanes.
People from more than eighty different countries died in the attacks.
Most of the victims were Americans.

The U.S. government asked other nations to join in a fight against terrorism
   around the world.
President Bush ordered air attacks against Afghanistan.
Then he sent American troops there to fight against the terrorist organization
   responsible for the attacks on the United States.

Check-Up

Events in History

| Great Society   House of Representatives   March on Washington   Gulf War   Watergate |

1. Martin Luther King, Jr., led the _____ in 1963.

2. President Nixon resigned because of a political scandal called _____.

3. President Johnson's _____ programs helped poor people.

4. In 1991 President Bush sent troops to fight in the _____.

5. The _____ impeached the president in 1998.

Did You Understand?

1. What was the civil rights movement?
2. Who was its most famous leader?
3. Who became the president in 1963 after an assassination?
4. Which president resigned because of a political scandal?
5. Which president was called "the great communicator"?

People In History

Fill in the correct answer.

1. _____ began relations with China.

2. _____ was assassinated in 1963.

3. _____ was a famous leader of the civil rights movement.

4. _____ was the president when terrorists attacked the United States in 2001.

5. _____ was impeached in 1998.

A. Are you ready for some questions about history and government?

B. Yes, I am.

A. Okay. What are the two major political parties in the United States today?

B. The _____ and the _____.

A. What's the most important right granted to U.S. citizens?

B. _____.

A. And can you tell me who Martin Luther King, Jr., was?

B. Yes. He was _____.

A. Which countries did we fight with in World War II?

B. I'm sorry. I'm not sure I understand the question. Do you mean which countries were our enemies, or which countries did we help?

A. Who did we help? Who were the Allies?

B. _____.

A. Good. And can you tell me who the president was during World War II?

B. Yes. It was _____.

Practice with another student. Take turns asking and answering the questions.

Review

Paired Questions

Ask and answer these questions. Practice with other students.

1. What national holiday do Americans celebrate at the beginning of September?
   What does this holiday celebrate?

2. Why is the United States called "a nation of immigrants"?
   Why do immigrants come to the United States?

3. What was the Great Depression?
   What happened during the Depression?

4. Which president had a plan called The New Deal?
   What happened under this plan?

5. When did the United States enter World War II?
   Who did the United States fight against during that war?

6. What is the UN?
   What happens at the UN?

7. Which two major countries competed during the Cold War?
   How were their political systems different?

8. What national holiday do Americans celebrate on the third Monday in January?
   What does this holiday celebrate?

9. What are some responsibilities of U.S. citizens?
   What is the most important right U.S. citizens have?

10. Which president resigned from office?
    Why did he resign?

11. Which president was impeached by the House of Representatives in 1998?
    Why was he impeached?

12. What happened on September 11, 2001?
    Who was the president on that date?

 **Review**

Talking Time Line: Important Dates in U.S. History

Write these events on the correct lines in the time line below.

> Martin Luther King, Jr., led a civil rights march in Washington.
> The Great Depression began in the United States.
> The House of Representatives impeached President Clinton.
> The United States entered World War I.
> World War II ended.
> Japan bombed Pearl Harbor.
> Terrorists attacked the World Trade Center and the Pentagon.

1900

—1917 _____ The United States entered World War I. _____

—1929 _____

—1941 _____

—1945 _____

1950

—1963 _____

—1998 _____

2000
—2001 _____

Now practice with another student, asking and answering questions based on the time line.

When did _____?

What happened in _____?

CHAPTER TEST

Choose the best answer.

Example: In the 1800s America grew very quickly because of

  (A) the Revolutionary War.
  ● the Industrial Revolution.
  (C) World War I.
  (D) the Depression.

A. COMPLETE THE SENTENCES

1. The telephone was an important American
   (A) organization.
   (B) depression.
   (C) invention.
   (D) demonstration.

2. Workers formed labor unions to
   (A) fight the Confederacy.
   (B) fight in the Union army.
   (C) move to farms.
   (D) make life better for factory workers.

3. The United States is often called a nation of
   (A) farmers.
   (B) immigrants.
   (C) factories.
   (D) voters.

4. Franklin D. Roosevelt was the president during
   (A) World War I.
   (B) World War II.
   (C) the Korean War.
   (D) the Vietnam War.

5. The Cold War ended when
   (A) many countries formed the United Nations.
   (B) President Nixon resigned.
   (C) the United States dropped atomic bombs on Japan.
   (D) the Soviet Union broke up into independent states.

6. The United States fought against Germany during
   (A) World War II.
   (B) the Vietnam War.
   (C) the Korean War.
   (D) the Gulf War.

7. After World War II, the United States fought Communist forces in
   (A) Vietnam and England.
   (B) Korea and Vietnam.
   (C) Korea and Australia.
   (D) Alaska and Hawaii.

8. Citizens can vote for the president
   (A) every 2 years.
   (B) every 4 years.
   (C) every 6 years.
   (D) every 8 years.

9. The president who resigned from office was
   (A) Richard Nixon.
   (B) Gerald Ford.
   (C) Lyndon Johnson.
   (D) Bill Clinton.

10. Martin Luther King, Jr., led the March on Washington in 1963 to support
    (A) the New Deal.
    (B) the Vietnam War.
    (C) new civil rights laws.
    (D) a new holiday in January.

11. Lyndon B. Johnson became the president when
    (A) Bill Clinton was impeached.
    (B) Richard Nixon resigned.
    (C) John F. Kennedy was assassinated.
    (D) Franklin D. Roosevelt died.

12. The United States entered World War II when the Japanese bombed
    (A) England.
    (B) Nagasaki.
    (C) the United Nations.
    (D) Pearl Harbor.

B. ANSWER THE QUESTIONS

13. Who served longer than any other U.S. president?
    - (A) Franklin D. Roosevelt.
    - (B) Ronald Reagan.
    - (C) Bill Clinton.
    - (D) Jimmy Carter.

14. What word describes the political system of the former Soviet Union?
    - (A) Democratic.
    - (B) Republican.
    - (C) Communist.
    - (D) Social Security.

15. What ISN'T a responsibility of U.S. citizens?
    - (A) To serve on a jury.
    - (B) To pay taxes.
    - (C) To obey laws.
    - (D) To work on a farm.

16. What DIDN'T happen during the Depression?
    - (A) Many people lost their jobs.
    - (B) Many banks closed.
    - (C) Many countries formed the UN.
    - (D) Many factories closed.

17. When did the United States and the Soviet Union compete?
    - (A) During the Civil War.
    - (B) During the Cold War.
    - (C) During the Revolutionary War.
    - (D) During World War II.

18. What was the name of Martin Luther King, Jr.'s, famous speech in 1963?
    - (A) The Gettysburg Address.
    - (B) The New Deal.
    - (C) A Nation of Immigrants.
    - (D) I Have a Dream.

19. Which event in U.S. history DIDN'T happen in the 1900s?
    - (A) The Civil War.
    - (B) The Depression.
    - (C) The Watergate scandal.
    - (D) The Vietnam War.

20. Which event in U.S. history DIDN'T happen in the 1800s?
    - (A) Francis Scott Key wrote the *Star-Spangled Banner*.
    - (B) The United States expanded to the Pacific Ocean.
    - (C) Abraham Lincoln signed the Emancipation Proclamation.
    - (D) The Social Security system began.

C. DICTATION

Listen and write.

1. _____

2. _____

3. _____

4. _____

5. _____

Civics Enrichment

Where do people in your community vote on Election Day? What happens at the polling places? What do the voting machines look like? What local officials do people vote for in your community? How do people register to vote? Get information from your local Board of Elections. As a class, visit a polling place on Election Day.

Biography Project: Write a short biography about a famous American—an inventor, a president, or someone else. Use your school library or local library to find information. Give a short presentation to the class.

Discuss: What are the rights and responsibilities of all people in their communities and in the nation? How are these rights and responsibilities different for citizens and non-citizens?

CHAPTER SUMMARY

KEY VOCABULARY

PEOPLE	EVENTS/HISTORICAL PERIODS	PLACES & COUNTRIES	VERBS	OTHER WORDS
actor		Afghanistan	acquit	administration
American	civil rights movement	Arlington, Virginia	assassinate	airplane
Bill Clinton	Cold War	Austria-Hungary	attack	Allied Nations
Black	Depression	Bosnia	celebrate	armed forces
candidate	election	Boston	choose	assassination
citizen	Election Day	China	collapse	atomic bomb
factory worker	Great Society	East Coast	compete	civil rights
family	Gulf War	England	count	communist
farmer	impeachment trial	Florida	crash	Democratic
Franklin D. Roosevelt	Industrial Revolution	France	die	demonstration
George Bush	Korean War	Germany	discuss	discrimination
George W. Bush	Labor Day	Hawaii	elect	equal rights
Gerald Ford	March on	Hiroshima	expand	expansion
immigrant	Washington	Italy	fight	human rights
Japanese	national holiday	Japan	hijack	immigration
Jimmy Carter	New Deal	Kosovo	impeach	labor union
John F. Kennedy	Operation Desert	Lincoln Memorial	improve	national debt
leader	Storm	Nagasaki	invent	peace
Lyndon B. Johnson	recession	New Jersey	kill	police department
Native American	Vietnam War	New York City	lead	politics
official	war	Pearl Harbor	lose	protest
President	Watergate	Pennsylvania	obey	railroad
Reverend Martin	World War I	Pentagon	pay	Republican
Luther King, Jr.	World War II	Russia	produce	salary
Richard Nixon		Somalia	raise	scandal
Ronald Reagan	INVENTIONS	Soviet Union	reduce	Social Security system
terrorist	cotton gin	United States	reform	social services
troops	light bulb	Vietnam	regulate	speech
Vice President	machine	Washington, D.C.	remember	stock market
victim	phonograph	West Coast	resign	taxes
worker	sewing machine	World Trade Center	shoot	terrorism
	telephone		spend	union
	typewriter		stop	United Nations (UN)
			support	vote
			take office	welfare system
			win	world power

APPENDIX

100 Questions for Review   199

Songs of Freedom   204

Pledge of Allegiance   207

Oath of Allegiance   207

Scripts for Listening Exercises   208

Sentences for Dictation Exercises   210

Index   212

Correlation Key   214

100 Questions for Review

Test yourself. Cover the answers and try to answer the questions. Then practice asking and answering these questions with other students.

1. What are the colors of our flag? — Red, white, and blue.

2. How many stars are there in our flag? — 50.

3. What color are the stars on our flag? — White.

4. What do the stars on the flag mean? — There is one star for each state in the Union.

5. How many stripes are there in the flag? — 13.

6. What color are the stripes? — Red and white.

7. What do the stripes on the flag mean? — They represent the original 13 states.

8. How many states are there in the Union? — 50.

9. What is the 4th of July? — Independence Day.

10. What is the date of Independence Day? — July 4th.

11. Independence from whom? — England.

12. What country did we fight during the Revolutionary War? — England.

13. Who was the first president of the United States? — George Washington.

14. Who is the president of the United States today? — _____

15. Who is the vice president of the United States today? — _____

16. Who elects the president of the United States? — The electoral college.

17. Who becomes president of the United States if the president should die? — The vice president.

18. For how long do we elect the president? — Four years.

19. What is the Constitution? — The supreme law of the land.

20. Can the Constitution be changed? — Yes.

21. What do we call a change to the Constitution? — An amendment.

22. How many changes or amendments are there to the Constitution? — 27.

23. How many branches are there in our government?

Three.

24. What are the three branches of our government?

Legislative, executive, and judiciary.

25. What is the legislative branch of our government?

Congress.

26. Who makes the laws of the United States?

Congress.

27. What is Congress?

The Senate and the House of Representatives.

28. What are the duties of Congress?

To make laws.

29. Who elects Congress?

The people.

30. How many senators are there in Congress?

100.

31. Can you name the two senators from your state?

_____

32. For how long do we elect each senator?

Six years.

33. How many representatives are there in Congress?

435.

34. For how long do we elect the representatives?

Two years.

35. What is the executive branch of our government?

The president, cabinet, and departments under cabinet members.

36. What is the judiciary branch of our government?

The Supreme Court.

37. What are the duties of the Supreme Court?

To interpret laws.

38. What is the supreme law of the United States?

The Constitution.

39. What is the Bill of Rights?

The first ten amendments to the Constitution.

40. What is the capital of your state?

_____

41. Who is the current governor of your state?

_____

42. Who becomes president of the United States if the president and the vice president should die?

The Speaker of the House of Representatives.

43. Who is the Chief Justice of the United States?

_____

44. Can you name the thirteen original states?

New Hampshire, Massachusetts, Rhode Island, Connecticut, New York, New Jersey, Pennsylvania, Delaware, Maryland, Virginia, North Carolina, South Carolina, and Georgia.

45. Who said, "Give me liberty or give me death"?

Patrick Henry.

46. Which countries were our enemies during World War II?

Germany, Italy, and Japan.

47. What are the 49th and 50th states of the Union?

Alaska and Hawaii.

48. How many terms can a president serve?

Two.

49. Who was Martin Luther King, Jr.?

A civil rights leader.

50. Who is the head of your local government?

_____

51. According to the Constitution, a person must meet certain requirements in order to be eligible to become president. Name one of these requirements.

A person must be a natural-born citizen of the United States.
A person must be at least 35 years old.
A person must have lived in the United States for at least 14 years.

52. Why are there 100 senators in the Senate?

There are two from each state.

53. Who selects the Supreme Court justices?

The president appoints them.

54. How many Supreme Court justices are there?

Nine.

55. Why did the Pilgrims come to America?

For religious freedom.

56. What is the head executive of a state government called?

The governor.

57. What is the head executive of a city government called?

The mayor.

58. What holiday was celebrated for the first time by the American colonists?

Thanksgiving.

59. Who was the main writer of the Declaration of Independence?

Thomas Jefferson.

60. When was the Declaration of Independence adopted?

July 4, 1776.

61. What is the basic belief of the Declaration of Independence?

That all people are created equal.

62. What is the national anthem of the United States?

The *Star-Spangled Banner*.

63. Who wrote the *Star-Spangled Banner*?

Francis Scott Key.

64.	Where does freedom of speech come from?	The Bill of Rights.
65.	What is the minimum voting age in the United States?	Eighteen.
66.	Who signs bills into law?	The president.
67.	What is the highest court in the United States?	The Supreme Court.
68.	Who was president during the Civil War?	Abraham Lincoln.
69.	What did the Emancipation Proclamation do?	It freed many slaves.
70.	What special group advises the president?	The Cabinet.
71.	Which president is called "the father of our country"?	George Washington.
72.	What form is used to apply to become a naturalized citizen?	Form N-400, "Application to File Petition for Naturalization."
73.	Who helped the Pilgrims in America?	The American Indians (Native Americans).
74.	What is the name of the ship that brought the Pilgrims to America?	The *Mayflower*.
75.	What were the 13 original states of the United States called?	Colonies.
76.	Name three rights or freedoms guaranteed by the Bill of Rights.	Freedom of speech. Freedom of the press. Freedom of religion. Freedom of assembly. The right to own a gun (bear arms). The government needs a warrant to search or take a person's property. A person may not be tried twice for the same crime, and does not have to testify against himself. The right to a trial, and the right to a lawyer. The right to a trial by jury.
77.	Who has the power to declare war?	The Congress.
78.	What kind of government does the United States have?	A democratic form of government. / A representative form of government. / The United States is a republic.
79.	Which president freed the slaves?	Abraham Lincoln.
80.	In what year was the Constitution written?	1787.

81. What are the first ten amendments to the Constitution called?	The Bill of Rights.
82. Name one purpose of the United Nations.	For countries to discuss and try to resolve world problems; to provide economic aid to many countries.
83. Where does Congress meet?	In the Capitol in Washington, D.C.
84. Whose rights are guaranteed by the Constitution and the Bill of Rights?	Everyone (citizens and non-citizens living in the United States).
85. What is the introduction to the Constitution called?	The Preamble.
86. Name one benefit of being a citizen of the United States.	Obtain federal government jobs; travel with a U.S. passport; petition for close relatives to come to the U.S. to live.
87. What is the most important right granted to U.S. citizens?	The right to vote.
88. What is the United States Capitol?	The place where Congress meets.
89. What is the White House?	The president's official home.
90. Where is the White House located?	Washington, D.C.
91. What is the name of the president's official home?	The White House.
92. Name one right guaranteed by the First Amendment.	Freedom of speech/press/religion/ assembly.
93. Who is the commander-in-chief of the U.S. military?	The president.
94. Which president was the first commander-in-chief of the U.S. military?	George Washington.
95. In what month do we vote for the president?	November.
96. In what month is the new president inaugurated?	January.
97. How many times may a senator be re-elected?	There is no limit.
98. How many times may a congressman or congresswoman be re-elected?	There is no limit.
99. What are the two major political parties in the United States today?	Democratic and Republican.
100. How many states are there in the United States?	50.

America the Beautiful

O beautiful for spacious skies,
for amber waves of grain,
For purple mountain majesties,
above the fruited plain!
America! America!
God shed His grace on thee,
And crown thy good with brotherhood,
from sea to shining sea.

America
(My Country 'Tis of Thee)

My country 'tis of thee,
Sweet land of liberty,
Of thee I sing;
Land where my fathers died,
Land of the Pilgrim's pride;
From every mountainside,
Let freedom ring.

The Star-Spangled Banner
(The National Anthem)

Oh, say, can you see,
by the dawn's early light,
What so proudly we hailed
at the twilight's last gleaming?
Whose broad stripes and bright stars,
through the perilous fight,
O'er the ramparts we watched,
were so gallantly streaming?
And the rockets' red glare,
the bombs bursting in air,
Gave proof through the night
that our flag was still there.
Oh, say, does that star-spangled
banner yet wave
O'er the land of the free
and the home of the brave?

A Better Life

I've come to make a better life.
This is my new home.
I'm so glad to be here.
I've come to make a better life.
And I hope one day
we can find a way
for everyone to live together.

I feel like a stranger here
in this new culture and new language.
Does anybody understand me?
Do they know the way I feel inside?
I miss my family and the friends I left behind.
I think about them all the time.

I'm called an immigrant.
Some people think I don't belong here.
But many generations past
have shared the dream I have —
To live in freedom and with dignity
in this land of peace and liberty.

I can't wait until the morning when
I take the oath to be a citizen.
Until that day there is so much to be done
I guess my journey's just begun.

Words of Freedom

Pledge of Allegiance

I pledge allegiance to the flag
of the United States of America,
and to the republic for which it stands,
one nation, under God, indivisible,
with liberty and justice for all.

Oath of Allegiance

(New citizens recite this oath of allegiance to the United States at their naturalization ceremony.)

"I hereby declare, on oath, that I absolutely and entirely renounce and abjure all allegiance and fidelity to any foreign prince, potentate, state or sovereignty, of whom or which I have heretofore been a subject or citizen; that I will support and defend the Constitution and laws of the United States of America against all enemies, foreign and domestic; that I will bear true faith and allegiance to the same; that I will bear arms on behalf of the United States when required by the law; that I will perform noncombatant service in the armed forces of the United States when required by the law; that I will perform work of national importance under civilian direction when required by the law; and that I take this obligation freely without any mental reservation or purpose of evasion; so help me God."

Scripts for Listening Exercises

Listen and circle the correct answer.

1. A. Could you spell your family name, please?
   B. M-A-R-T-I-N-E-Z.
2. A. Could you spell your last name, please?
   B. S-A-N-T-O-S.
3. A. Could you spell your surname, please?
   B. T-R-A-N.
4. A. How do you spell your last name?
   B. C-R-U-Z.
5. A. How do you spell your family name?
   B. W-O-N-G.

Chapter A – Page 7

Listen and write the name you hear.

1. A. What's your family name?
   B. Garcia.
   A. Could you spell that, please?
   B. G-A-R-C-I-A.
2. A. What's your last name?
   B. Lam.
   A. Could you spell that, please?
   B. L-A-M.
3. A. What's your surname?
   B. Perez.
   A. Could you spell that, please?
   B. P-E-R-E-Z.
4. A. What's your last name?
   B. Cheng.
   A. How do you spell that?
   B. C-H-E-N-G.
5. A. What's your family name?
   B. Velasquez.
   A. How do you spell that?
   B. V-E-L-A-S-Q-U-E-Z.
6. A. What's your surname?
   B. Gudarski.
   A. Please spell it.
   B. G-U-D-A-R-S-K-I.

Chapter A – Page 11

Listen and circle the number you hear.

1. My address is thirty Main Street.
2. My address is thirteen Spring Street.
3. My address is fifty Stanley Avenue.
4. My address is forty-six fifteen Donaldson Street.
5. My address is eighteen thirty-nine Parkman Avenue.
6. My address is eight forty-two Conway Avenue.

Chapter B – Page 30

*Listen carefully and circle **A** or **B**.*

1. Where were you born?
2. What's your date of birth?
3. What's your place of birth?
4. When were you born?
5. Where are you from?
6. What's your birth date?

Chapter 1 – Page 41

*Listen and circle **A**, **B**, or **C**.*

1. What's the name of your state?
2. Name the capital of the United States.
3. What's the name of your state capital?
4. What state do you live in?
5. Name the capital of your state.
6. What's the capital of the United States?

Chapter 2 – Page 54

Listen and circle the correct answer.

1. How many states are there in the United States?
2. How many stripes does the American flag have?
3. How many colors does the American flag have?
4. What were the first thirteen states called?
5. What are the colors of the American flag?
6. What colors are the stripes on the flag of the United States?

Chapter 3 – Page 66

Listen and circle the correct answer.

1. Where does the president work?
2. Where does the Congress work?
3. Who makes the laws of the United States?
4. Who explains the laws of the United States?
5. Who enforces the laws of the United States?
6. Who works in the Congress of the United States?

Chapter 4 – Page 79

*Listen and circle **A**, **B**, or **C**.*

1. Who's the Commander-in-Chief of the armed forces?
2. Who works in the Congress of the United States?
3. Who explains the laws of the United States?
4. Who works in the White House?
5. Who makes the laws of the United States?
6. Who don't the American people elect?

Chapter 5 – Page 95

These questions sound the same, but they are very different. Listen carefully and circle the correct answer.

1. What's the highest court in the United States?
2. What's the highest law in the United States?
3. What are the three levels of government in the United States?
4. What are the three branches of the United States government?
5. Which branch of government enforces the laws?
6. Which branch of government explains the laws?

Chapter 6 – Page 105

Listen and circle the correct answer.

1. Where was the first American colony?
2. When did people from England come to the first American colony?
3. When did the Pilgrims come to America?
4. Why did the Pilgrims come to America?
5. What is the name of the colony that the Pilgrims came to?
6. What is the name of the ship that the Pilgrims sailed to America?

Chapter 7 – Page 125

Listen and circle the correct answer.

1. When did the colonists sign the Declaration of Independence?
2. Where did the colonists sign the Declaration of Independence?
3. Why did the colonists sign the Declaration of Independence?
4. Who did the colonies fight against during the Revolutionary War?
5. When did the colonies fight the Revolutionary War?
6. Why did the colonies fight the Revolutionary War?

Chapter 8 – Page 148

*Listen carefully and circle **A** or **B**.*

1. Who is the president of the United States?
2. Who was the first president of the United States?
3. Who was the commander-in-chief of the armed forces?
4. Who is the commander-in-chief of the armed forces?
5. Who works in the executive branch of the government?
6. Who worked in the executive branch of the government?
7. Who's the chief executive?
8. Who was the chief executive?

Chapter 9 – Page 166

*Listen carefully and circle **A**, **B**, **C**, or **D**.*

1. Who was the first president of the United States?
2. Who was the president during the Civil War?
3. Who wrote the Declaration of Independence?
4. Who's the president of the United States?
5. Who was the third president of the United States?
6. Who is called "the father of our country"?

Chapter 10 – Page 181

Listen and circle the correct answer.

1. Who was the president during World War II?
2. When did the United States enter World War II?
3. What two countries became major world powers after World War II?
4. Which countries did the United States fight against during World War II?
5. What new international organization was formed after World War II?
6. What happened during the Depression?

Sentences for Dictation Exercises

Chapter A – Page 17

1. My name is _____.
2. This is my home.
3. This is my address.
4. The United States is my new home.
5. I want to be a citizen.

Chapter B – Page 33

1. I am from _____.
   (name of country)
2. My home is in _____.
   (name of city or town)
3. I am living in the United States of America.
4. This is my telephone number.
5. I want to be a citizen of the United States.

Chapter 1 – Page 47

1. The United States is a large country.
2. I live in a big city.
3. The capital of the United States is Washington, D.C.
4. I believe in the Constitution of the United States.
5. Texas is a large state.

Chapter 2 – Page 57

1. There are fifty (50) states in the United States.
2. The American flag has three (3) colors.
3. The flag is red, white, and blue.
4. The flag of the United States has thirteen (13) stripes.
5. There are fifty (50) stars on the flag.

Chapter 3 – Page 69

1. The president of the United States lives in the White House.*
2. The White House is in Washington, D.C.
3. The Congress of the United States makes the laws.
4. The U.S. government has three branches.
5. Washington, D.C. is the capital of our country.

Chapter 4 – Page 83

1. The president and the vice president work in the White House.
2. I'm studying about the president of the United States.
3. There are one hundred (100) senators.
4. The Supreme Court explains the laws.
5. We elect a president every four years.

Chapter 5 – Page 97

1. I am studying the Constitution of the United States.
2. There are twenty-seven (27) amendments to the Constitution.
3. The first ten (10) amendments are the Bill of Rights.
4. The Constitution gives rights to all people in the United States.
5. The first amendment gives Americans freedom of speech.

Chapter 6 – Page 115

1. Columbus sailed to America in 1492.
2. The first American colony was in Virginia.
3. The Pilgrims came to America in 1620.
4. Thanksgiving is an American holiday in November.
5. The first thirteen (13) states were called colonies.

Chapter 7 – Page 133

1. The colonists didn't like English laws.
2. Thomas Jefferson wrote the Declaration of Independence.
3. The colonies signed the Declaration of Independence in 1776.
4. The Fourth (4th) of July is America's birthday.
5. Independence Day is a summer holiday.

* In these dictation exercises, the words "president" and "vice president" can be spelled with either lower-case or upper-case initial letters.

Chapter 8 – Page 151

1. The Constitution is the highest law in the land.
2. The Constitution gives many powers to the Congress.
3. George Washington was the first president of the United States.
4. Americans vote for the president in November.
5. Congress has the power to declare war.

Chapter 9 – Page 169

1. America's national song is about the flag.
2. The Constitution of the United States has twenty-seven (27) amendments.
3. Abraham Lincoln was the president during the Civil War.
4. The Civil War was a war between the North and the South.
5. Presidents' Day is a national holiday in February.

Chapter 10 – Page 195

1. The first Americans were farmers.
3. Many factory workers got hurt.
3. Immigrants came from many different countries.
4. The United States has a democratic system of government.
5. The most important right citizens have is the right to vote.

Index

A

"A Better Life," 206
Afghanistan, 188, 189
Alaska, 156
Aldrin, Buzz, 55
Allied nations, 178
Alphabet, 6
Amendments, 93, 144, 164
"America," 113, 204
"America the Beautiful," 45, 204
Arlington, Virginia, 155, 188, 189
Armstrong, Neil, 55
Astronauts, 55
Atlantic Ocean, 35, 37
Atomic bomb, 178
Austria-Hungary, 177

B

Bates, Katharine Lee, 45
Beliefs, 42
Bill of Rights, 93, 144, 164
Bosnia, 188
Boston Tea Party, 118
Branches of government, 59, 60, 64, 71, 81, 138
Bush, George, 187
Bush, George W., 188, 189

C

Cabinet, 139
California, 156
Canada, 35, 37
Capitol, U.S., 62, 138
Carter, James Earl, 186
Chief Justice, 77
China, 186
City manager, 88
Civil rights movement, 182, 183
Civil War, 158–160
Clinton, William J., 188
Cold War, 179
Colonies, 50, 103, 110, 118, 120, 122
Colorado, 45
Columbus, Christopher, 100

Commander-in-Chief, 75, 139
Confederacy, 158–159
Congress, 62, 72, 74, 138
Connecticut, 110
Constitution, 92, 136, 138, 143–144, 164

D

Declaration of Independence, 122, 124, 126
Delaware, 110
Democratic form of government, 86
Democratic Party, 184
Depression, 177–178

E

Election, 2001, 188
Emancipation Proclamation, 160
England, 103, 118, 122, 154, 156, 177–178
Executive branch, 59, 60, 62, 64, 71, 75, 138–140
Expansion, 156

F

Factories, 172
First Amendment, 144
Flag, U.S., 49, 50, 53
Florida, 156, 188
Ford, Gerald, 186
Fourth of July, 128
France, 156, 177

G

Georgia, 110
Germany, 177, 178
Gettysburg Address, 162
Governors, 88
Great Depression, 177–178
Great Society programs, 185
Gulf War, 187

H

Hawaii, 156, 178
Henry, Patrick, 118
House of Representatives, 72, 74, 138

I

"I Have a Dream" speech, 183
Immigrants, 175
Impeachment, 188
Income taxes, 164
Independence Day, 128
Independence Hall, 122, 126
Industrial Revolution, 172
Inventions, 172
Italy, 178
Iwo Jima, 55

J

Jamestown, 103, 113
Japan, 178
Jefferson, Thomas, 122, 126
Johnson, Lyndon B., 185
Judicial branch, 59, 60, 62, 64, 71, 77, 138, 140

K

Kennedy, John F., 185
Key, Francis Scott, 154
King, Rev. Martin Luther, Jr., 182, 183
Korean War, 179
Kosovo, 188

L

Labor Day, 173
Labor movement, 173
Labor unions, 173
Legislative branch, 59, 60, 62, 64, 71, 72, 138
Levels of government, 88
Lincoln, Abraham, 159, 160, 162
Local government, 88
Louisiana Purchase, 156

M

Map, U.S., 36–37
March on Washington, 182, 183
Marines, 55
Maryland, 110
Massachusetts, 103, 110, 113, 118

Mayflower, 103, 113
Mayors, 88
Mexico, 35, 37, 156
Mississippi River, 156
Months of the year, 19, 25
"My Country 'Tis of Thee,"
    113, 204

N

National anthem, 154, 155, 205
Native Americans, 100, 107
New Deal, 178
New Hampshire, 110
New Jersey, 110, 189
New York, 110
New York City, 55, 188, 189
Nixon, Richard, 186
North Carolina, 110
Numbers, 8, 10, 165

O

Oath of Allegiance, 207
Operation Desert Storm, 187
Ordinal numbers, 165
Oregon Country, 156

P

Pacific Ocean, 35, 37
Pearl Harbor, 178
Pennsylvania, 110, 189
Pentagon, 155, 188, 189
Permanent resident card, 4, 8
Philadelphia, 118, 122, 126,
    136, 147
Pike's Peak, 45
Pilgrims, 103, 107, 113
Pledge of Allegiance, 55, 207
Plimoth Plantation, 113
Plymouth, 103, 107
Preamble, 143
President, 60, 62, 75, 139–140
Presidents' Day, 160

R

Reagan, Ronald, 187
Representative form of
    government, 86
Representatives, 60, 62, 64, 72,
    138
Republic, 86
Republican Party, 184
Revolutionary War, 120, 122,
    136, 147
Rhode Island, 110
Roosevelt, Franklin Delano, 178
Russia, 156, 177, 178

S

Senate, 72, 74, 138
Senators, 60, 62, 64, 72, 138
September 11, 2001, 55, 188,
    189
Slavery, 158–160
Social security card, 8
Social security system, 178
Somalia, 188
Songs
    "A Better Life," 206
    "America" ("My Country
        'Tis of Thee"), 113,
        204
    "America the Beautiful,"
        45, 204
    "Star-Spangled Banner,"
        154, 155, 205
South Carolina, 110
Soviet Union, 179
Spain, 100, 156
"Star-Spangled Banner," 154,
    155, 205
State government, 88
Succession, presidential, 140
Supreme Court, 60, 62, 77,
    140, 188

T

Terms of office, 72, 75, 81, 138,
    140
Terrorist attack, 55, 155, 188,
    189
Texas, 156
Thanksgiving, 107, 113

U

Union, 158–159
Unions, 173
United Nations, 179

V

Vice president, 60, 62, 75,
    139–140
Vietnam War, 179, 185, 186
Virginia, 103, 110, 113, 155,
    188, 189
Vote, Right to, 164, 184
Voting, 184
Voting age, 164

W

War of 1812, 154
Washington, George, 120, 147,
    160
Washington, D.C., 37, 62, 189
Watergate, 186
White House, 62, 75
World Trade Center, 55, 188,
    189
World War I, 177
World War II, 55, 178

CORRELATION KEY

Voices of Freedom	Foundations (Student Book & Workbook)	Word by Word Basic	Word by Word	Side by Side (3rd edition)	Side by Side Interactive CD-ROM / Side by Side TV Video	ExpressWays Book 1 (2nd edition)	Access
Chapter A	Chapter 1	pp. 2–7, 48, 54–55	pp. 1–3, 30, 33	Book 1: Chapters 1–3	Level 1A: Segments 1–4	Chapter 1	Chapters 1, 2
Chapter B	Chapter 1	pp. 2–7, 48, 54–55	pp. 1–3, 30, 33	Book 1: Chapters 4–6	Level 1A: Segments 5–8	Chapter 1	Chapters.3, 4
Chapter 1	Chapter 2	pp. 8–11, 167–171	pp. 4–9	Book 1: Chapters 9, 10	Levels 1A & 1B: Segments 13–15	Chapter 2	
Chapter 2	Chapters 3, 9	pp. 12–17, 98–109	pp. 10–11, 56–61	Book 1: Chapters 7, 8	Level 1A: Segments 9–12	Chapter 4	
Chapter 3	Chapter 4	pp. 18–29, 40–45	pp. 13–18, 25–27	Book 1: Chapter 11	Level 1B: Segments 16, 17	Chapter 3	
Chapter 4	Chapter 5	pp. 52–53, 146–149	pp. 32, 84	Book 1: Chapter 12	Level 1B: Segments 18, 19	Chapter 5	
Chapter 5	Chapter 6	pp. 56–67	pp. 34–39	Book 1: Chapters 13, 14	Level 1B: Segments 20–23	Chapter 5	
Chapter 6	Chapter 8	pp. 76–81	pp. 44–49	Book 1: Chapter 15	Level 1B: Segment 24	Chapter 6	
Chapter 7	Chapter 10	pp. 110–113	pp. 66–67	Book 1: Chapter 16	Level 1B: Segment 25	Chapter 6	
Chapter 8	Chapter 11	pp. 114–127	pp. 68–74	Book 1: Chapter 17	Level 1B: Segment 26	Chapter 7	
Chapter 9	Chapter 12	pp. 128–137	pp. 75–78	Book 2: Chapters 1–3	Level 2A: Segments 27–32	Chapter 7	
Chapter 10	Chapter 13	pp. 138–149	pp. 80–85	Book 2: Chapters 4, 5	Level 2A: Segments 33–36	Chapter 8	

This correlation key indicates textbook lessons that are topically or grammatically related to the instruction in each chapter of *Voices of Freedom* and complement the English and civics curriculum.

Foundations is a pre-beginner's all-skills textbook that offers basic vocabulary and language practice through interactive and communicative activities, games, and exercises.

The **Word by Word Basic** and **Word by Word** Picture Dictionaries present essential words for students' everyday language needs through full-color illustrations and an interactive methodology combining communicative and all-skills practice.

Side by Side is a 4-level textbook series offering all-skills practice through a general language development curriculum based on English grammar and vocabulary.

The **Side by Side Interactive** CD-ROM Program offers interactive exercises that integrate video, audio, graphics, and text and includes check-up tests and lifeskills/civics lessons. The **Side by Side TV** Video Program provides video-based instruction and all-skills practice through accompanying workbooks.

ExpressWays is a 4-level textbook series offering all-skills practice through a competency-based curriculum integrating lifeskills, grammar, and functions of English.

Access, an all-skills text for students with limited literacy skills, offers basic reading and writing practice that supports the instruction provided through the first two chapters of *Voices of Freedom.*